THE
NEW HEART
MATTERS

THE
NEW HEART
MATTERS

A COVENANT JOURNEY

LORRAINE
KELLEY BULLOCK

K KUDU
PUBLISHING

Thanks

To God "to the praise of His glorious grace, which
He has freely given us in the Beloved One."

To Daddy and Mother Dear—who raised our
family under a covenant of loving devotion.

To my husband, Lionel, for his continuous support.
He is a good and faithful steward over his life,
his family, his duties, and his possessions.

To Leon, Sr. my late husband and our five children:
Andrea, Leon, Jr., LaVaughan, Adrienne, and Allison
and their families who keep their father's saying alive.

To my siblings and their families: Dr. Russell V. Kelley Jr.
(Maryland State Senator Delores Kelley, Retired), Ms.
Lillian K. Pierce, Mrs. Denise K. Vice (Nathan), and Darryl
A. Kelley, Esq. (Evelyn, Esq.) for their ongoing support

To Rev. Delores Edwards, Dr. Jacqueline Moore, Rev. Yvonne
Alexander, and Ms. Mary Urquhart for reading the first draft
of The New Heart Matters and offering valuable feedback.

To Bishop B. Courtney McBath for his generosity
awarded me through his abundance of encouragement.

To the KUDU Book Team for reaching their goal of
successfully publishing my book. To God be the glory!

CONTENTS

FAMILY AND FRIENDS' COMMENTS

Note: Thanks to my nephew David B. Kelley, owner of DBK Studios, LLC, for providing a narration of the prologue for this book, *The New Heart Matters*.

Regarding the narration of the prologue and feedback from the draft copy:

"The dictation of your prologue was spot-on. Although deep and intriguing, it was articulated well with calm tones. The reader and listener (audience) will be well-pleased with the description and overtone of his voice. I can't wait to read your book. I know it will be well-received by everyone and loved for its ease of reading with imperative principles and teaching of LOVE from the Bible."

—ADRIENNE, DAUGHTER, NORFOLK, VA

"Hey MeMa, I finally listened to the prologue for your book. It's wonderful. *The New Heart Matters*—I love it. Can't wait to read the rest of it."

—ALEYSHIA, GRANDDAUGHTER, NORWICH, CT

"Finally listened to this segment of your life aka *A New Heart Matters,* and MAAAAAAAAAAAAAA, you are miraculous, gifted, talented, and blessed! I can't wait until it's all done. This is life for so many in our community. It gave me a sense of worth and culture."

—ALLISON, DAUGHTER, NORFOLK, VA

"WOW! I just listened to it, and it was so uplifting to my spirit. It gave details about your life growing up, and I could actually see it happening. David's voice and music will put you at ease. Ma, that was so great! Thanks for sharing."

—LEON JR., SON, NORFOLK, VA,

"@Leon DITTO! It was the story of not only who Ma is but the story of who we are!"

—ANDREA, DAUGHTER, VIRGINIA BEACH, VA

"Definitely takes you on a ride of memories and makes you feel like you were right there."

—LAVAUGHAN, SON, NORFOLK, VA

"*The New Heart Matters* is a physical manifestation of what it looks like to commit to a lifelong pursuit of God's heart. My grandmother has dedicated her life to knowing God just a little bit more each day no matter the season, no matter her age—a newer, ever-evolving heart is always attainable."

— ANDRE, GRANDSON, CHICAGO, IL

"First time, I listened. Second time, I took notes. I am now digesting. Well done, Lorraine."

—STEPHEN BULLOCK, COLUMBIA, MD

"Lorraine, Lorraine! Beautiful. Your life story was interesting, and the ending *testimony* was so touching. I was in tears. God has really blessed you and is using you to bless others. Hallelujah! Praise God! David did a great job."

—LUCRETIA SINGLETON, CHESAPEAKE, VA

"*The New Heart Matters* is speaking to us at such a pivotal time in America. It is apparent that we have strayed far away from the covenant. New hearts and right minds will help to restore our relationship with God. I have read some parts over and over and over because it speaks to the truth. The book also requires us to self-check."

—Ms. MARY URQUHART, CHESAPEAKE, VA

"Your teaching is so valid and needed for us older believers. It reminds us of sinfulness and righteous living and how they begin in the heart. For all of us, teaching about sin and dishonorable living is needed in today's 'Shoot 'Em Up, Bang Bang' society."

—DR. JACQUELINE MOORE, NORFOLK, VA

"I closed my eyes as the words led me through each scene, feeling honored that I could witness a snippet of each character's life. Each scene transitioned smoothly into the next, in time with the gentle music underneath.

I realized I was viewing the scenes in sepia, as though watching a film, until your aunt looked outside and saw the blades of grass, at which point vibrant colors suddenly appeared.

Goodness, what a beautifully written piece! I imagined a cinematic journey of a proud, hard-working family, well-respected in the community.

I loved the way you delivered it—enough gravitas and emotion to draw the listener into the story though not too much *emotive modulation*. It allows the listener to visualize it as a 'story of the past' rather than your own interpretation. A definite *sweet spot* which I loved!"

—KAREN COOPER, NOTTINGHAM, UNITED KINGDOM

"My dear Lorraine—Thank you for sharing the prologue for your new book. I felt and experienced a journey from the past. I imagined grand ole Shiloh Baptist Church as a bright beacon to the community—your father providing a clothes-cleaning establishment service for Norfolk residents and your mother as the helper and queen of the family. The vividness of your new birth was relatable and inspirational. Can't wait to see the published memoir."

—DR. WINIFRED PHILLIPS, CHESAPEAKE, VA

"Hi, Aunt Lorraine. It was my pleasure and a true honor to record the prologue of your book *The New Heart Matters*. Your words brought memories of happiness and family bonding to me that seem missing in today's time. This is how our God works—through each gift as a collective being, one with our talents to better humanity. What an authentic experience! I look forward to recording the entire novel."

—DAVID, NEPHEW, MEMPHIS, TN

"Dear Lorraine—You who are my 'special childhood friend' of seventy-eight years. It all started at Shiloh Baptist Church at the age of two in your mother's Sunday class. After that, it was kindergarten at a Presbyterian Church, then elementary and junior high school at which time we started a social and savings club. Lastly, we attended Booker T. Washington High School. You have always had God's glow and a kind spirit."

—ESTELLE EDMONDS BUSSEY, CHESAPEAKE, VA

"Again tonight, I was listening to your story that David recorded. Thank you for sharing it with us. I was truly blessed. It reminded me of what family should be like today. To hear how your father and mother raised you—God first, wife, family, and business—made me think of how family life should be. I didn't know that Huntersville was that well-established, with so many family-owned businesses and the community working together.

What a blessing to be raised in a godly home and to hear about the fact that when your dad worked, your mom worked at the shop, and when you and your siblings all came home from school, you took over.

There is much that we all need to hear. Please keep writing. I pray that you can turn this into a play so that many young people and older as well can hear and see what it was like back then and can be like that or even better today. We need to be reminded of how families should be and love each other. I just wanted to share my heart. I even Googled to see what Huntersville was like back then—one word: *unique*!

'Be blessed!'"

—Sharon Peet, Norfolk, VA

"Lorraine—As one of the coworkers with whom you shared your born-again experience well over fifty years ago, I am totally excited about this prologue. You have given others a pictorial walk through your life with God and a view of the Holy Spirit leading you as you have expressed your faith in Jesus Christ. What a testimony! I leave this thought: 'Blessed are those who trust in the Lord and have made the Lord their hope and confidence.' —Jeremiah 17:7 (NLT)"

—Cora E. Bridgers, Virginia Beach, VA

"Lorraine—This narration of the prologue is awesome! I would like to chat with you about it."

—Rev. Yvonne Alexander, Chesapeake, VA

"Lorraine, Lorraine, Lorraine—The prologue touched my mind and my heart in a powerful, loving, and tender way. Thank you for a wonderful, accommodating, fulfilling, and happy visit through Huntersville before integration. Your clarity about your life and Christian journey makes me even more thankful that you are my friend, soul-sister in Christ, prayer warrior, and confidant. You reaffirmed in me the 'urgency of now' as we study God's Word and

lovingly with determination work His battlefield. Love you dearly. Thumbs up. The prologue is amazing. This book is a must-read."
—Barbara Saulsbury, Virginia Beach, VA

"Hi, Lorraine. What an awesome testimony. Your prologue brought back so many memories of growing up in Huntersville. To God be the glory for the great things He has done!"
—Rosemary Zinnanti, Norfolk, VA

"Mrs. Lorraine—Listening to this prologue again has blessed me tremendously. It has reinforced the importance of having structure, order, and faith in our Lord Jesus Christ. The adjectives used to describe the different events provided me with a clear picture. Keep up your excellent work, MeMa!"
—Nicole J. Ballou, Norfolk, VA

"This prologue provides a great introduction to what you will encounter while reading *The New Heart Matters*. It invoked childhood memories and provided a memorable description of the neighborhood while reviewing historical moments from this author's perspective. The narrator's had great voice inflections and smooth transitions from point to point. I can't wait to read this book!"
—Denise Kelley Vice, Sister, Midlothian, VA

"This narration of the prologue provided wonderful highlights and informative moments of the author's early life and her life going forward. It shows how this family worked together. The voice quality of the reader was enticing. The pronunciations were clear, and the story showed clear continuity and was smooth from beginning to end."

—NATHAN VICE, BROTHER-IN-LAW, MIDLOTHIAN, VA

"Timing is everything! I am glad that I came home within the time span of the writing of *The New Heart Matters: A Covenant Journey* by Lorraine Bullock. I am thoroughly impressed by her workmanship, dedication, and commitment. I am sitting here with the author as I write, and I feel blessed to call her a friend and woman of God. When God spoke, she listened and handled the task with an open heart. Those who read the book will find words of encouragement to lean on when life is good and when life is not so good. I can't wait to add Lorraine's book to my most treasured book collection."

—JOE JAMES, AUTHOR, WRITER, ACTOR, DIRECTOR, NEW YORK, NY

A SPECIAL SECTION OF WRITINGS BY THE AUTHOR

THE GIFT OF LOVE BUNDLED TOGETHER IN FAMILY

The New Heart Matters: A Covenant Journey was inspired by an encounter I had while quiet before the Lord. I sensed God's voice speaking the word "covenant" in my heart and knew that God, by His Spirit, was leading me on a promised-land journey to find out the biblical meaning of covenant and to know God as a covenant God.

This book talks about God's love and His acceptance of believers into His family. As God's children, they are blessed with the gift of covenant love. God's love is spread throughout the new hearts of the believers by the Holy Spirit and is secured there by Jesus Himself. He is the fulfillment of all the covenant promises. In Psalm 89:28 (ISV), God says, "I will show my gracious love toward him forever, since my covenant is securely established with him."

In the appendix, you will find the section titled "The Gift of Love: Bundled Together in Family." I have included prayers, poems, special celebration greetings and other written thoughts of and for my family. I used the following theme—Family Memories—and have written from the view of a widow, a mother, a grandmother, and a wife.

God's Love—Covenant Love—Family Love.
These three,
Bundled together in unity!

"I will give you a new heart and put a new spirit in you; I will remove from you your heart of stone. . . . And I will put my Spirit in you and move you to follow my decrees."
—EZEKIEL 36:26-27 (NIV)

PROLOGUE:
MY CONVERSION

I was born in the early 40s in Norfolk, Virginia. My parents, Russell (See Note A: "My Father, A Servant Leader" on page 79.) and Fannie Kelley, raised my siblings and me in the Huntersville section of the city. It was during the time of segregation when the races were separated. Only black families lived in the community.

Huntersville was a lively and busy place filled with a variety of stores; small grocery stores usually located on various street corners with apartment complexes above the store, confectionary stores with many sweets—candy bars, lollipops, all kinds of chips and ice cream cones and snow cones, a general market, and a family-owned market. There were other businesses in the community, including a restaurant, laundromat, shoe shop, fish market, pharmacy, hair salons, barbershops, and a post office substation. Connected to the post office was Sears Arena, where concerts, dances, and parties were held.

There were two clothes cleaners, and my father owned one. The family referred to it as The Shop. My family lived about a block and a half from the cleaners. Most of the business owners lived in Huntersville, and many of their family members worked with them. While my father was at work during the day at the naval yard in Portsmouth, my mother managed the shop, and my siblings and I would release her when we got out of school.

I was twelve years old when I started "going to take care of the shop." When people brought their clothes to be cleaned, I would write up a ticket for them with their names and the pieces of clothing they were leaving and then get the clothes ready to be taken to the main station for cleaning by tagging and placing them in the designated spots for pickup.

I knew how to manage money for when people came to get their clothes. They would hand me their ticket, and I had to look among the hanging clothes, find the ones with the matching ticket number, and give them to the customer. They would then pay for our service, and with "Thank you," they would leave. One thing that I find memorable was the sign on the wall near the front counter of the shop that read: "Service with a Smile."

ONE THING THAT I FIND MEMORABLE WAS THE SIGN ON THE WALL NEAR THE FRONT COUNTER OF THE SHOP THAT READ: "SERVICE WITH A SMILE."

When my mother left the shop in the evening, she would go home and prepare dinner for the family, and when my daddy arrived home from work around five o'clock in the evening, dinner was served. After dinner, my father would go to the shop and relieve whoever was there. He would close at 8 p.m.

Along with the businesses throughout Huntersville, there were schools, a library, the Young Women's Christian Association (YWCA), and a variety of churches. Our family were members of Shiloh Baptist Church, located three blocks from my father's shop. In 1949, the church left the community and moved about three miles away to a new location in the Brambleton section of the city. Our family remained faithful members of Shiloh. My father was a deacon there. He was very active in the Laymen's League and held an office in the Lott Carey Baptist Foreign Mission, now a global Christian organization. My father displayed great leadership in the community. During the late 50s and early 60s, he was the president of the PTA at John T. West Elementary School and, later, Booker T. Washington High School.

In the community, my father served as president of the Huntersville Model City Commission from 1971-1975 and was treasurer of the Norfolk Citizen Participation Council, Inc., from 1974 until 1983. During that time, he also served as the first vice president of the Norfolk Inner-City Federal Credit Union and president of the Huntersville Civic League. My father was highly respected throughout the city and at his job. People would seek him out for advice regarding many issues. I was once told by one of our family's church friends how my father had influenced his life. He said that he had been involved in worldly activities, but my father would often talk to him regarding a change needed in his life. When he shared that story with me, he, along with his wife, were dedicated Christians and quite active members serving at Shiloh Baptist Church.

Needless to say, our family was known as "Christian people." As children and teenagers, we attended Sunday school regularly, and on Sunday evenings, we attended the Baptist Training Union (BTU). During the summer, we went to Bible school, and during special holidays, Christmas, and Easter, we participated in plays and other activities. We were all baptized by the age of twelve. My siblings and I had a stable upbringing and were taught to love others and show respect to our elders by using our manners, greeting others as we approached or saw them, saying, "Thank you," when given something, or giving up our seat if needed.

While talking recently to my childhood friend Shirley, she told me that she often thinks about how she started going to church. She said that when she was twelve years old and I was thirteen, she asked me where I go to church. I told her, and she said that she wanted to start going to church too. I told her about our church bus and the pickup time for Sunday school. Shirley showed up and became a regular member of the Sunday school class. Today, she remains faithful to her Christian faith.

I married in 1963, and eight years later, my husband and I had two children. After the birth of my second child, my life changed in a dramatic way. Although I had been baptized when I was about nine years old, twenty years later, I had a conversion experience. I was born again. I was at home watching a talk show on a Christian network where guests were invited to share testimonies, stories, news, and music from a Christian perspective. There were times when well-known ministers would share the Word. I noticed that the hosts, as well as the guests, seemed full of joy and happiness as they talked about and shared the good news about Jesus Christ. Many guests shared their conversion experiences. I began to want and desire such an experience. It became clear to me that I needed to repent of my many sins and ask Jesus to come live in my heart. I wanted to be saved. I wanted Jesus to be my Savior and Lord.

The hosts of the 700 Club, the talk show that I was looking at, encouraged viewers who had given their hearts to the Lord to call the CBN station to share with the program hosts their testimony regarding inviting Jesus Christ into their hearts. I did, and I was overjoyed! I remember how excited I was to hear the host announce that a young lady from Norfolk had called to share that she had just given her life to the Lord.

My heart changed instantaneously, and I didn't just feel it—I knew it in my soul. That was the beginning of me having a sense in my heart that God was speaking to me. I was led to take my Bible with me when I left the living room to go to my bedroom. I sat on the side of the bed and opened the Bible. There I saw Psalm 40. It began, "I waited patiently for the LORD to help me, and he turned to me and heard my cry. He lifted me up from the pit of despair, out of the miry clay; He set my feet upon a rock, and made my footsteps firm" (Psalm 40:1-2, NLT). There was absolutely no doubt in my mind that God had heard my plea for Him to come to dwell in my heart, and He did!

WHEN I GAVE MY LIFE TO THE LORD, MY HEART CHANGED INSTANTANEOUSLY, AND I DIDN'T JUST FEEL IT—I KNEW IT IN MY SOUL.

I woke up the next morning to newness. The breath of life was fresh like newly washed linens—airy. The curtains at my kitchen window were golden yellow like the bright morning sun, and as I looked out of the window, the blades of grass were standing at attention, outfitted in green coverings, blade by blade, hosting the early morning dew. I will never forget that vivid picture of my newness. I was a new creation and a brand new man; old things had passed away. I was born again. That was fifty years ago, and that newness remains because God did it, and I am grateful!

I shared my born-again experience with many people. I called my parents and told them how God had touched my life and brought about a marvelous change when I invited Him to dwell in me. I told my siblings, and they said, "Oh, that's great!" I told some of my coworkers at school that I had been saved. I confessed Jesus as Lord at church during testimonial services. My conversion experience was such a vivid experience, and it brought about immediate and lasting change. Jesus clearly said in John 3:7 (NIV, emphasis added): "YOU MUST BE BORN AGAIN." This was after He had said, "Very truly I tell you, no one can see the kingdom of God unless they are born again. . . . No one can enter the kingdom of God unless they are born of water and the Spirit" (John 3:3 and 5, NIV).

In the mid-70s, while praying in the Spirit using unknown tongues, the Lord gave me, for I sensed it in my spirit, an acronym for the word FAITH: **F**ather, **A**ll's **I**n **T**hy **H**and. I have shared this phrase in many ways: by word of mouth, on note cards, on bags, and on the cover of a journal that I created.

In 2008, I wrote a book about my grandson titled, *MeMa, It's Anointing Time*. It tells how the Lord spoke to my heart about anointing various parts of his body as I put lotion on him. For example, after his morning shower, I would say as I placed lotion on his hands, "Today, I anoint Alvin's hands as he picks up his dirty socks and clothes that have been thrown all over his bedroom floor.... Lord, I speak to Alvin's chest, the place where we find his heart. Lord, let Alvin's heart beat to the sound of love."

In 2011, while on my knees in my office and quiet before the Lord, I sensed one word beating loudly in my heart. It was the word covenant, and I believe God sent me on a covenant journey. It is now ten years later, and I am still on this writing journey. I've named it *The New Heart Matters*.

I believe the covenant is a divine pledge or promise, coming directly from God in which He binds Himself in relationship to believers in His Son and vows to keep and fulfill His promises and offer blessings to them through His Spirit. Seeing the covenant from this view helped me to desire a closer bonding with the Father to better know Him and Christ Jesus, who is our eternal life.

MY HOPE IS TO ENCOURAGE
READERS TO DISCOVER THE POWER
OF THIS COVENANT OF LOVE.

My hope is to encourage readers to discover the power of this covenant of love. God promised to remove the believer's sinful heart and to give him a new heart and a new spirit by which the sinful nature of life is taken away and God gives the believer the gift of the Holy Spirit and transforms him into the likeness of Jesus. This new life comes directly from God. This new heart beats first and then the new creation is birth. This person is born again. The believer becomes a brand-new creation. As Christians, we recognize and live with power over the sinful nature. We live and walk daily in the Spirit and are assured that we have spiritual power to say, "No!" to worldly ways and worldly activities. As believers, we die to ourselves, and Jesus lives His life through us. We know and are assured that the new heart matters, for God's presence and Jesus's life dwell there.

God is a God of love, and He is faithful to love those who believe in Him. In Psalm 89:28 (NIV), the writer points to this everlasting love: "I will maintain my love to him forever, and my covenant with him will never fail."

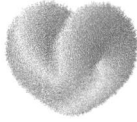

INTRODUCTION:
A PROMISED LAND JOURNEY

SEEKING TO KNOW GOD AS MY COVENANT
GOD BY KNOWING HIS COVENANT
PROMISES AND CONFIDENTLY BELIEVING
AND RECEIVING THESE COVENANT
GIFTS OF GRACE THAT I MAY BECOME
A PARTAKER OF HIS DIVINE NATURE

P eace can be established when two or more parties come together in a bonding relationship. This is what a covenant does; it creates a bond of relationships. Our God is a covenant God who desires fellowship with mankind. He loves us with a love that's forever—a love that never, never, never fails.

> IN PSALM 89:28 (NIV) THE WRITER POINTS
> TO THIS EVERLASTING LOVE: "I WILL
> MAINTAIN MY LOVE TO HIM FOREVER, AND
> MY COVENANT WITH HIM WILL NEVER FAIL."

I want to know more about God's covenant that's written about throughout the Bible. More than that, I want to know God as my covenant God and to understand and embrace His covenant promises.

Let me share with you the reason why. I mentioned in the prologue that one evening about ten years ago, I was drawn in my study to spend a quiet time before the Lord. While on my knees, in complete quietness, I began to sense the word covenant in my spirit. Just a few years earlier, my sister Lillian, two close friends, and I had participated in a book talk discussion using Chuck Swindoll's book *David*.[1] We read and talked about the ark of the covenant and understood that the different items in the ark and the ark of the covenant itself had a deeper spiritual meaning. (See Note B: "What is the Ark of the Covenant?" on page 85.) Matthew Henry says, "The Mosaic covenant points out Christ as our Light, and as the Bread of life to our souls."[2]

Other than that, I had not paid much attention to the word covenant. Before leaving my study, I knew that the Holy Spirit was pointing me towards a "promised land" journey—the study

---

1 Charles R. Swindoll, *David: A Man of Passion & Destiny* (Anaheim, CA: Insight for Living, 1997.)
2 Matthew Henry "Hebrews 9 Commentary," *Hebrews 9 Commentary (Matthew Henry)*, www. kingjamesbibleonline.org/Hebrews-9_Commentary-Henry/.

of the covenant made by God to humanity that He would forgive sin and restore fellowship with humanity.[3]

3   "What Is the Ark of the Covenant?" GotQuestions.*Org*, 25 June 2010, www.gotquestions.org/ark-of-the-covenant.html.

CHAPTER 1

GOD'S DIVINE COVENANT

AN AMAZING GRACE

"Know therefore that the Lord your God, He is God, the faithful God, who keeps His covenant and His lovingkindness to a thousand generations with those who love Him and keep His commandments."
—DEUTERONOMY 7:9 (NASB)

O ur God is a faithful God. He has bound Himself in relationship through covenant and lovingkindness to those who love Him and believe in His Son, Jesus Christ who is Himself called a covenant. (See Isaiah 42:6 and Isaiah 49:8.) God sustains that relationship through offering divine promises and ensuring that the promises and blessings are fulfilled. God does this through His amazing grace. Grace is couched in the center of this divine covenant promise.

"The Word became a human being and made his dwelling
among us. We have seen his glory, . . . of the one and only Son,
who came from the Father, full of grace and truth."
—JOHN 1:14 (CEV)

GOD DEMONSTRATES HIS GRACE WHICH REIGNS IN THE NEW HEART IN EXCEEDINGLY GREAT WAYS.

God demonstrates His grace which reigns in the new heart in exceedingly great ways through Jesus Christ:

» His kindness towards us. (Ephesians 2:7)
» Our redemption through His blood. (Ephesians 1:7)
» The forgiveness of our sin. (Ephesians 1:7)
» Salvation given through faith. (Ephesians 2:8)
» God's acceptance of us because of our faith in His Son. (Romans 3:22)
» His righteousness given as a gift to us as believers. (Romans 3:22-24)
» His blessings and promises of the covenant of grace. (Gill's exposition on Isaiah 49[4])

Murray writes in his book *The Two Covenants*:

We have found that the central blessing of the New covenant, flowing from Christ's redemption and the pardon of

---

4 John Gill, "Isaiah 49 Commentary - John Gill's Exposition of the Bible," *Biblestudytools.Com*, www.biblestudytools.com/commentaries/gills-exposition-of-the-bible/isaiah-49/.

our sins, is the new heart in which God's law, and reverence and love have been put. [5]

In John 17:24 (NLT), Jesus tells of the love His Father had given him before the creation of the world:

"Father, I want these whom you have given me to be with me where I am. Then they can see all the glory you gave me because you loved me even before the world began!"

Charles Spurgeon said in his sermon "Love" that we love Him because He first loved us, and in that first love, there is the pledge and promise that He will love us even to the end.[6] I believe that the covenant is a divine promise/pledge, coming directly from God, in which He binds Himself in a love relationship to believers through Jesus Christ and vows to keep them, fulfill His promises, and offer blessings to them. This divine covenant and pledge is a gift of grace, showing that God loves us unconditionally. (See Note C: "The Covenant—A Gift of Love" on page 87.)

This love is from Him to man.

John 3:16 (NLT) tells about God loving the world: "For this is how God loved the world: He gave His one and only Son, so that everyone who believes in him will not perish but have eternal life."

God's giving of His Son to the world was a great sacrificial act of love. This act flowed out of the heart of God.

---

5 Andrew Murray, *The Two Covenants* (Scotts Valley, CA: CreateSpace, 2020) 77.
6 Charles Spurgeon, "Love," *The Spurgeon Center*, 19 Dec. 1858, www.spurgeon.org/resource-library/sermons/love/#flipbook/.

> GOD'S GIVING OF HIS SON TO THE
> WORLD WAS A GREAT SACRIFICIAL
> ACT OF LOVE. THIS ACT FLOWED
> OUT OF THE HEART OF GOD.

In *The Two Covenants*, Andrew Murray wrote about the meaning of grace and its relationship to love. He stated that grace is "the disposition in God that moves Him to love us freely without our merit and to bestow all His blessings upon us."[7]

In his book, *Marriage Covenant*, Dr. Fred Lowery writes:

> "Covenant was in the heart of God from the day he created mankind. It is a term that describes God's unique relationship with his people and carries with it the guarantee of all the benefits and blessings of that relationship. Covenant is how he chose from the beginning of time to demonstrate his love and his desire to fellowship with his creation."[8]

And Murray points out that "The central thought of the covenant is that the heart is to be put right and equipped to know God."[9]

Love was to be spread abroad throughout the heart of mankind by the Holy Spirit.

---

7 Andrew Murray, *The Two Covenants*, 78.
8 Fred Lowery, *Covenant Marriage: Staying Together for Life* (New York, NY: Simon Schuster, 2002),
9 Andrew Murray, *The Two Covenants*, 77.

CHAPTER 2

GOD'S COVENANT

PROMISES AND BLESSINGS

"He has given us his precious and very great promises, so that
through them you may become partakers of his divine nature."
—2 PETER 1:4 (ESV)

Father All's In Thy Hand is an acronym that the Lord spoke in my heart in the late 1970s to describe the word faith. It's a short statement to declare daily and throughout the day. For me, it means that everything is in God's hands. It is definitely linked to God taking care of all things for those who love Him, believe, and trust in Him and His Son, Jesus Christ. He uses the Holy Spirit to accomplish the work. Job 12:10 (NLT) states, "The life of every living thing is in His hand."

> GOD'S PROMISES GIVE LIGHT AND
> REVELATION OF THE WORK THAT THE
> HOLY SPIRIT HAS DONE, IS DOING,
> AND WILL DO IN OUR NEW HEARTS.

Andrew Murray mentioned in *The Two Covenants* how covenant is used in a meaningful way to help grow our faith. God's covenant is full of many wonderful and magnificent promises to those who are in covenant with Him. The promises give light and revelation of the work that the Holy Spirit has done, is doing, and will do in our new hearts. These promises are used to stir up, build, and sustain our faith in God as these promises are fulfilled. They reveal what God intends to bring about in those who know and recognize Him as their covenant-keeping God. God's promises are for all who have faith.

The Word says that all God's promises are found in Jesus, and these promises are secure in him and fulfilled through him:

> "For all of God's promises have been fulfilled in Christ with a resounding, "Yes!" and through our "Amen" (which means "Yes") ascends to God for His glory." —2 Corinthians 1:20 (NLT)

As a believer, I want to understand the importance of God's promises in my Christian walk because faith points to trusting His promises. This thought brings me back to the acronym Father All's In Thy Hand and reminds me to trust God in all things; trusting in His promises assures us that through Jesus Christ, they will be fulfilled. God is faithful to the promises found in His Word!

"But the Scriptures say that sin controls everyone, so that God's promises will be for anyone who has faith in Jesus Christ."
—GALATIANS 3:22 (CEV)

Let me share with you a few of God's promises that were fulfilled in my born-again conversion experience and some of the blessings that I received. As mentioned before, I grew up going to church, participating in Christian activities, and getting baptized when I was nine years old. However, it was twenty years later that I was born again. I desired to know Jesus in a personal way. I confessed the many sins I committed throughout my life—lying, cheating, immorality, smoking, etc.—and God forgave me.

He promises in 1 John 1:9 (NIV): "If we confess our sins, He is faithful and just to forgive us our sins and to cleanse us of our sins and to cleanse us from all wickedness." I repented, turned away from those sins, and asked God to come dwell in my heart.

HE PROMISES IN 1 JOHN 1:9 (NIV): "IF WE CONFESS OUR SINS, HE IS FAITHFUL AND JUST TO FORGIVE US OUR SINS AND TO CLEANSE US OF OUR SINS AND TO CLEANSE US FROM ALL WICKEDNESS."

God promises in Ezekiel 36:26 (NLT): "I will give you a new heart and put a new spirit in you. I will take out your stony, stubborn heart and give you a tender, responsive heart."

After responding by repenting and asking God to come dwell in my heart, He accepted me (justification). My heart was now a dwelling place for God and His Son. The Lord Jesus Christ's presence is there.

Romans 10:9 (ESV) admonishes us to "Confess with our mouth Jesus is Lord and believe in our heart that God raised him from the dead and you will be saved."

Jesus fulfilled that in me. I am saved.

I believed the promise in 2 Corinthians 5:17 (ESV), "Therefore if anyone is in Christ, he is a new creation. The old has passed away. Behold, the new has come!"

I was excited and joyful about knowing and believing God's promises in His Word.

I was grateful for the promise in Romans 5:5 (NIV) that "God's love has been poured out into our hearts through the Holy Spirit, who has been given to us."

Galatians 4:6 (NIV) tells us that "God sent the Spirit of His Son into our hearts."

I was quite conscious of this newness—the Holy Spirit dwelling in my heart. The night that I was saved, I was led by the Spirit to read Psalm 40:1-2 in the Bible. This was certainly a brand new experience, and it was a signal to me that God, by His Spirit, was guiding me. God had touched my life!

That same night, I was delivered from smoking. I had the habit of smoking a pack of cigarettes a day. I've not picked up a cigarette since then. That was well over fifty years ago.

The next morning the curtains at my kitchen window seemed to shine with a brilliance of light, and the grass outside of my apartment looked as if the blades of grass were at attention with beads of morning dew lingering on top.

I was more than excited about sharing my testimony of how God had come into my life with others. I told my parents, my siblings, my friends, my coworkers, and many church members.

Jesus tells of this promise in Matthew 10:32 (NLT): "Everyone who acknowledges me publicly here on earth, I will acknowledge before my Father in heaven."

THERE IS HEALING IN THE WORK OF THE CROSS.

I've been healed! The cross that Jesus died on has healing in it. In the early 70s, I was healed of Bell's palsy, a condition that paralyzed the left side of my face and caused me to speak with a slur. Within six months, God healed me! In 2009, I was diagnosed with breast cancer, had surgery, and five years later, was free of the horrific disease. There is healing in the work of the cross.

Isaiah 53:5 (KJV) points out a promise of healing:

> "He was wounded for our transgressions, he was bruised for our iniquities: the chastisement of our peace was upon him; and with his stripes we are healed."

There are many more promises that God, through the Lord Jesus Christ, has fulfilled in my life, and to them, I say, "Amen!"

CHAPTER 3

LOOKING BACK TO THE BEGINNING

"In the beginning, God created...."
—GENESIS 1:1 (NIV)

God created the heavens and the earth. In the beginning, there was darkness as black as coal—a vastness of pitch black—and God spoke light: stars and moons, lights of the night and light for the day. A wide span of beautiful blue sky with a bright golden sun shooting rays that reached every crack and crevice stretched overhead. God formed every mountain high and every valley low on the earth to house the land-like ripples of ups and downs that would one day carry the paths where many feet would tread. He created the beast of the field and the birds of the air, flitting and flying and flapping their wings gracefully, looking and eye-spying a place to land safely. God created the waters of the sea as a home for whales and squid and tuna, the chicken-of-the-sea; these waterways housed goldfish and starfish and seahorses aplenty. Plants lived there too—water lilies, seaweeds, and lily pads as resting places for frogs, dragonflies, and mosquitoes.

Nehemiah declared, "You alone are the Lord. You made the heavens, even the highest heavens, and all their starry host, the earth and all that is on it, the seas and all that is in them" (Nehemiah 9:6, NIV).

GOD SAID THAT IT IS ALL VERY GOOD!

God said that it is ALL very good!

Regarding Adam's image in Genesis 1:26 (author paraphrase), God then said, "Let us make Adam from the *red dust* of the earth (*Hitchcock's Bible Names Dictionary*[10]), and let's make him like us, in our image, with a divine nature—*truly righteous and holy* (Ephesians 4:24, NLT)." *Matthew Henry's Concise Commentary* of Genesis 1:26 says it this way: "It is the soul, the great soul of man, that especially bears God's image."[11]

Man was made upright. In *John Gill's Exposition of the Bible*, Gill writes about the uprightness King Solomon talked about in Ecclesiastes 7:29. Gill says that the uprightness refers to Adam's

10   Roswell D. Hitchcock, "Adam," *Hitchcock's Bible Names Dictionary* (Grand Rapids, MI: Christian Classics Ethereal Library).
11   Matthew Henry, "Genesis 1 Bible Commentary" *Christianity*, www.christianity.com/bible/commentary/matthew-henry-complete/genesis/1.

"disposition of his mind not the stature of his body," for God is Spirit.[12] He continues his writing about Adam's uprightness:

> The powers and faculties of the soul of man, as they were when he was created; his understanding clear of all errors and mistakes, either about divine or human things; his affections regular and ordinate, no unruly passion in him, no sinful affection, lust and desire; he loved God with all his heart and soul, and delighted in him, and communion with him . . . and during his state of integrity, was pure and sinless.[13]

So God created man upright (Ecclesiastes 7:29), and Genesis 1:27 (NIV) states, "Male and female He created them." Jesus talked about the male and female in Matthew 19:5 (CEV) when the Pharisees tried to test him: "Don't you know in the beginning the Creator made a man and a woman? That's why a man leaves his father and mother and gets married."

(See Note D: "Marriage and My Upbringing" on page 91.)

After Adam was created, God breathed life into him, and he "became a living soul," according to Genesis 2:7 (ASV). Adam was placed in the Garden of Eden and, there, had the work of naming every animal. He was given "dominion over the earth" (Genesis 1:26, KJV) and directed not to eat "from the tree of the knowledge of good and evil" (Genesis 2:17, BSB). This is known as the Edenic covenant. The Edenic covenant (innocence) outlined man's responsibility toward creation and God's directive regarding the tree of knowledge of good and evil.[14]

---

12 John Gill, "Ecclesiastes 7:29—Bible Verse Meaning and Commentary," *Biblestudytools*, www.biblestudytools.com/commentaries/gills-exposition-of-the-bible/ecclesiastes-7-29.html.
13 John Gill, "Ecclesiastes 7:29—Bible Verse Meaning and Commentary."
14 "The Edenic Covenant," *GotQuestions*, 23 Nov. 2011, www.gotquestions.org/Edenic-covenant.html.

Regarding Genesis 2:7, John Gill stated that Adam had two natures: "the soul and body of man, the one is material and mortal, the other immaterial and immortal."[15]

God wanted a helper for Adam, so he formed woman from the rib of Adam's body. *Matthew Henry's Concise Commentary* says that since there was no sin in Adam, he felt no pain as God took the helper from his body. This was an act of grace.[16]

ADAM'S HEART KNEW NO SIN; THEREFORE, HE WAS NOT AFRAID.

Adam's heart knew no sin; therefore, he was not afraid. Death did not plague him; he experienced no suffering, pain, sickness, death, trials, poverty, hurt, hatred, harm, or shame. Matthew Henry stated, "Our first parents needed no clothes for covering against cold or heat, for neither could hurt them," for they were in a state of innocence.[17]

---

15 John Gill, "Ecclesiastes 7:29—Bible Verse Meaning and Commentary."
16 Matthew Henry, "Genesis 2 Bible Commentary," *Christianity*, www.christianity.com/bible/commentary/matthew-henry-concise/genesis/2.
17 Matthew Henry, "Genesis 2 Bible Commentary."

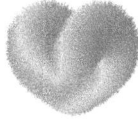

CHAPTER 4

THE BIRTH OF DISOBEDIENCE

"But you must not eat from the tree of the knowledge of good and
evil, for when you eat from it you will certainly die."
—GENESIS 2:17 (NIV)

A dam didn't remain innocent for long, for he disobeyed God's first command—neither to eat of nor touch the tree planted in the middle of the garden. This is known as the Adamic covenant (Genesis 3:16-19). The Adamic covenant (grace) included the curses pronounced against mankind for the sin of Adam and Eve as well as God's provision for that sin (see Genesis 3:15).[18]

God told Adam and Eve in Genesis 2:17 (ESV) that "in the day that you eat of it you shall surely die." As a result of their disobedience, Adam and Eve knew and experienced the shame

---

18 "What is the Adamic Covenant?" *GotQuestions*, 11 Nov. 2005, www.gotquestions.org/Adamic-covenant.html.

of nakedness. They tried to cover up with fig leaves (Genesis 3:7), but God had a better covering for their nakedness—animal skins (Genesis 3:21). Hebrews 9:22 says that without the shedding of blood, there is no cover for sins.

> ## JESUS IS THE PERFECT COVERING—THE ONE WHO COVERS US AND CLOTHES US WITH RIGHTEOUSNESS.

I believe God was pointing to His Son, Jesus, who would shed His blood on the cross for the sins of mankind. Jesus is the perfect covering—the one who covers us and clothes us with righteousness. When Adam sinned, mankind became a fallen people. Adam's heart knew deceit, and he turned away from God. Paul says that by the disobedience of one man, all were made sinners (Romans 5:19).

In Andrew Murray's *Abide in Christ,* he wrote, "Sin had disturbed all our relations; we were out of harmony with ourselves, with men, and with God."[19]

Adam's disobedience, this sin, was the cause of the evil that spread abroad in the heart of man. *Gill's Commentary* described the results:

> And so sinning, they lost the knowledge they had; their righteousness and holiness, the rectitude of their nature; the moral freedom of their will to that which is good, and their

---

19 Andrew Murray, *Abide in Christ* (Overland Park, KS: Digireads Publishing, 2019) 31.

power to perform it; and they lost the presence of God, and communion with him.[20]

And so it was darkness without God.

Sin is in man's nature. Consider what Paul says to the Ephesians:

> Once you were dead because of your disobedience and your many sins. You used to live in sin, just like the rest of the world, obeying the devil . . . He is the spirit at work in the hearts of those who refuse to obey God." —Ephesians 2:1-2 (NLT)

And Jesus told His disciples in John 14:17 (NIV), "The Spirit will show you what is true. The people of this world cannot accept the Spirit, because they can't see or know him."

Now, consider how many people live today:

» Lying and being dishonest—especially during tax season.
» Being selfish and wanting to be first on the highway or in the classroom.
» Cussing, fussing, and gossiping.
» Wanting what someone else has—clothes, tennis shoes, a car, or a house—being like the Joneses.
» Being jealous about someone's job position or just plain jealous.
» Committing fornication and/or adultery.
» Wanting someone's boyfriend or girlfriend—going as far as indulging fleshy desires housed in their bodies and minds.
» Disobeying their parents or breaking the law.
» Fighting with siblings and sometimes their friends.
» Stealing from those closest to them or robbing others in the community.

20 John Gill, "Ecclesiastes 7:29—Bible Verse Meaning and Commentary."

- » Kidnapping children.
- » Drinking and driving.
- » Drug dealing.
- » Taking a person's life given to them by God—massive killings.

SIN COMES FROM THE UNREGENERATE HEART.

These sins come from the unregenerate heart, and Jesus said, as written in John 8:7 (NIV): "Let any one of you who is without sin be the first to throw a stone."

Paul, the apostle, declared in Romans 6:23 (NIV), "For the wages of sin is death." We are all guilty of sinfulness, but Spurgeon, in his sermon "Christ in the Covenant," said that "the Mediator, who with mercy in his hands, came down to tell sinful man the news that grace was promised in the eternal counsel of the Most High."[21]

Paul told the people of Ephesus, "For by grace are we saved through faith ... and this is not from yourselves, it is the gift of God" (Ephesians 2:8, NIV). Matthew Henry agreed with him in his Ephesians 2:13 commentary: "*Salvation is far from the wicked*; but God is a help at hand to his people."[22]

---

21 Charles Spurgeon, "Christ in the Covenant," *The Spurgeon Center*, 31 Aug. 1856, www.spurgeon.org/resource-library/sermons/christ-in-the-covenant/#flipbook/.
22 Matthew Henry, "Ephesians 2 Bible Commentary," *Christianity*, www.christianity.com/bible/commentary/matthew-henry-complete/ephesians/2.

CHAPTER 5

BROKEN FELLOWSHIP

"The Lord saw that the wickedness of man was great in the earth, and that every imagination of the thoughts of his heart was only evil continually."
— GENESIS 6:5 (KJV)

Before the snake showed up in Eden, Adam and Eve enjoyed fellowship with God. They knew His presence. God gave Adam commands to follow. Adam disobeyed. The fellowship which the couple had with God was broken, and they were separated from Him.

ADAM AND EVE NO LONGER KNEW
THE RIGHT WAY TO LIVE AND
BEGAN THEIR JOURNEY OF LIFE
DOWN A DESTRUCTIVE PATH.

Adam and Eve no longer knew the right way to live and began their journey of life down a destructive path. As a result of this disobedience, sin fell on all humanity. This sin cut off the relationship between Adam and God. It brought death to mankind.

After the fall, all humanity was sinful. All human beings are born with and through a sinful nature. Our hearts are deceitful and wicked, and our lives are full of pride and all manner of evilness. (See Note F: "All Manner of Wickedness Found in Everyday Life" on page 101.)

In his book *The Complete Book of Bible Promises*, J. Stephen Lang asks, "Are there any sinners around anymore?"[23] He continues, "People are called dysfunctional or not in touch with themselves or negative or uptight or immature—but never sinful . . . The Bible assures us that we all sin."[24] Sin refers to a universal condition: focusing on ourselves instead of on God and other people. Our sin causes a separation between humanity and God. We need to be reconciled to God.

In his book *Living @ the Next Level*, B. Courtney McBath writes, "God made a way for us to escape the death of separation from Him."[25] McBath is referencing Romans 6:23 (NLT), "For the wages of sin is death, but the free gift of God is eternal life in Christ Jesus our Lord." He continues with the following:

> When we are separated from God, we experience a spiritual death. That is because God never intended for us to live separated from him—he created us to walk with him in a loving, fulfilling friendship. Though Adam and Eve's sin

23   J. Stephen Lang, *The Complete Book of Bible Promises* (Wheaton, IL: Tyndale House, 1997).
24   J. Stephen Lang, "Sin and Redemption," *CBN*, 15 Jan. 2023, www2.cbn.com/article/sin/sin-and-redemption.
25   B. Courtney McBath, Living @ the next Level: Transforming Your Life's Frustrations into Fulfillment Through Friendship with God (Brentwood, TN: Howard Books, 2010).

disconnected all of us from that friendship, God made a way to heal the breach and reconcile us back to himself. That way is Jesus Christ.[26]

(See Note E: "Just Because of Jesus" on page 97.)

---

26 B. Courtney McBath, *Living @ the Next Level.*

CHAPTER 6

THE NEW HEART—A NEW NATURE—A NEW LIFE

"I will give you a new heart and put a new spirit in you: I will remove
from you your heart of stone and give you a heart of flesh."
—EZEKIEL 36:26 (NIV)

G od's plan was to give man a new heart through His Spirit. From the beginning of the world, God knew that He would have a plan to bring mankind back to Himself, for He knew that man would need a Savior. This plan would be a covenant of love—a covenant of grace. (See Note G: "The Covenant of Grace" on page 107.) In His covenant plan, God declared that He would give mankind a new spirit and a tender, responsive heart:

"This is the covenant I will make with the people of Israel after that time," declares the Lord. "I will put my law in their minds and write it on their hearts. I will be their God, and they will be my people." —Jeremiah 31:33 (NIV)

FROM THE BEGINNING OF THE WORLD, GOD KNEW THAT HE WOULD HAVE A PLAN TO BRING MANKIND BACK TO HIMSELF, FOR HE KNEW THAT MAN WOULD NEED A SAVIOR. THIS PLAN WOULD BE A COVENANT OF LOVE—A COVENANT OF GRACE.

God made it possible for the believer in His Son, Jesus Christ, to be born again and receive a new life from Him. (See Note H: "Born Again" on page 109.) This new life is in Christ, and the Holy Spirit is in you to convey to you all that is in Christ. Christ lives in you through the Holy Spirit. John 3:1-8 describes a nighttime conversation between Jesus and the Jewish leader Nicodemus. Nicodemus had concerns of his own soul and its salvation, and *Matthew Henry's Concise Commentary* describes Jesus's instructions to him:

> Our Savior spoke of the necessity and nature of regeneration or the new birth, and at once directed Nicodemus to the source of holiness of the heart.[27]

In his book *The Spiritual Man*, Watchman Nee tells about regeneration or being born again. He writes, "The concept of

27 Matthew Henry, "John 3 Commentary," *Biblestudytools*, www.biblestudytools.com/commentaries/matthew-henry-concise/john/3.html.

regeneration as found in the Bible speaks of the process of passing out of death into life."[28] In Romans 5:21 (NLT), Paul writes, "So just as sin ruled over all people and brought them to death, now God's wonderful grace rules instead." And Timothy says this in 2 Timothy 1:9-10 (NIV):

> He has saved us and called us to a holy life—not because of anything we have done but because of his own purpose and grace. This grace was given us in Christ Jesus before the beginning of time, but it has now been revealed through ... Christ Jesus, who has destroyed death and has brought life and immortality to light through the gospel.

Man's sins would be forgiven. This believer would be given a new nature—a divine nature. This believer would be known as a new creation—a brand new man—for along with his forgiven sins, he would have power over his sinful nature through the Holy Spirit. As Christians, we are made by God to be holy.

Believers are told in 1 Peter 1:15 (NLT), "But now you must be holy in everything you do." First Corinthians 1:30 points out that in Christ, we are made holy and have been given a new heart and a new nature. Old things have passed away, according to 2 Corinthians 5:17, and things have become new—a new being, a new life, a new nature, new thoughts, new behaviors, and new principles and practices. We have been born anew. We now have a new spiritual life, that life is in Christ Jesus, and it's eternal.

---

28 Watchman Nee, *The Spiritual Man* (Anaheim, CA: Living Stream Ministry, 1998).

WE HAVE BEEN BORN ANEW. WE NOW
HAVE A NEW SPIRITUAL LIFE, THAT LIFE
IS IN CHRIST JESUS, AND IT'S ETERNAL.

"For the law of the Spirit of life [which is] in Christ Jesus
[the law of our new being] has set you free."
—ROMANS 8:2 (AMP)

New Life Through the Spirit

"Therefore there is no condemnation for those who are in Christ
Jesus, because the law of the Spirit of life (spiritual nature) set
me free from the law of sin and death (sinful nature)."
—ROMANS 8:1-2 (AUTHOR PARAPHRASE)

» Man is sinful;
» He is living by a sinful nature;
» God condemns sin;
» A sin offering is needed;
» God intervenes because He loves the world;
» God sends Jesus in the likeness of sinful man to be a sin offering;
» The new heart is given, and the sinful stony heart is removed by God the moment this man believes (Ezekiel 36:26);
» God offers righteousness for everyone who believes and has faith in Jesus Christ, the Son of God;

» This righteousness is by the word of faith that we proclaim (The word is near you; it is in your mouth and in your heart.);

» "If you confess with your mouth that Jesus is Lord and believe in your heart that God raised him from the dead, you will be saved" (Romans 10:9, ESV);

» "For it is with your heart that you believe and are justified, and it is with your mouth that you confess and are saved" (Romans 10:10, NIV);

» Everyone who calls on the name of the Lord will be saved (Joel 2:32 and Acts 2:21).

CHAPTER 7

GRACE GIVEN BEFORE TIME BEGAN

"This grace was given us in Christ Jesus before the beginning of time."
—2 TIMOTHY 1:9 (NIV)

Before the foundation of the world (see 1 Peter 1:20, Matthew 25:34, Acts 13:48, Ephesians 2:10; and 2 Thessalonians 2:13), there was a meeting of the council of the holy ones (Psalm 89:7). God had a meeting in the heavenly realms (Ephesians 1:3).

I BELIEVE GOD MET WITH HIS ONLY
BEGOTTEN SON AND HIS HOLY SPIRIT TO
DISCUSS A FEW MATTERS—IN PARTICULAR,

THE IMAGE IN WHICH MANKIND WOULD BE MADE AND THE SENDING OF CHRIST TO EARTH WITH AN ETERNAL GIFT TO BE OFFERED TO ALL MANKIND.

I believe God met with His only begotten Son and His Holy Spirit to discuss a few matters—in particular, the image in which mankind would be made and the sending of Christ to earth with an eternal gift to be offered to all mankind.

The Pulpit Commentaries for Ephesians 1:4 describes it this way:

> The Father chose the heirs of salvation . . . not after man had fallen, but before the foundation of the world. . . . Before even the world was formed mankind presented themselves to God as lost; the work of redemption was planned and its details arranged from all eternity.[29]

Gill's Commentary tells about Adam's image in Genesis 1:26:

> A consultation is held among the divine Persons about the formation of him [Adam] . . . it being proposed he should be made not in the likeness of any of the creatures already made, but as near as could be in the likeness and image of God.[30]

The council's discussion also included the elect—those who would receive God's gift of eternal salvation as an eternal inheritance. (See John 17:9 and 24 and John 6:39.) Titus 1:2 (NLT) describes them: "This truth gives them confidence that they have

29 "Ephesians 1 - the Pulpit Commentaries - Bible Commentaries." *StudyLight.Org*, www.studylight.org/commentaries/eng/tpc/ephesians-1.html.
30 John Gill, "Genesis 1:26 - Bible Verse Meaning and Commentary," *Biblestudytools.Com*, www.biblestudytools.com/commentaries/gills-exposition-of-the-bible/genesis-1-26.html.

eternal life, which God—who does not lie—promised them before the world began."

Matt Slick's publication of covenant, referring to the eternal covenant, says:

> In this covenant, God the Father and the Son made an agreement regarding the elect. This covenant was made before the universe was created, and it consisted of the Father promising to bring the Son all whom the Father had given him.[31]

The Pulpit Commentary for Colossians 3:12 describes the covenant with the elect: "This covenant was made known to God's elect among the twelve tribes: but being mystically understood, includes both Jews and Gentiles ... Israel not after the flesh, but after the Spirit."[32] The apostle Paul talks specifically about Gentiles being part of the elect:

> I Paul ... for the sake of you Gentiles ... God's grace that was given to me for you, that is, the mystery made known to me by revelation ... my insight into the mystery of Christ. ... That now has been revealed by the Spirit to God's holy apostles. ... This mystery is that through the gospel the Gentiles are heirs together with Israel, members together of one body, and sharers together in the promise in Christ Jesus.— Ephesians 3:1-6 (BSB)

The Godhead team worked proactively and created a strategic plan to address the future issues of mankind. They named the plan the covenant of Grace, and Christ was, at that time, set up as the mediator of it: from the promises of it in which were made

---

31 Matt Slick, "Covenant," *Christian Apologetics & Research Ministry*, 8 Dec. 2020, carm.org/christianity/covenant/.
32 "Colossians 3 - the Pulpit Commentaries - Bible Commentaries," *StudyLight.Org*, www.studylight.org/commentaries/eng/tpc/colossians-3.html.

before the world began; and from the spiritual blessings of grace in it which were given to God's elect before the foundation of it.

God established the covenant of grace to bless His creation and reconcile them back to Himself. He would demonstrate His love for them through His covenant plan and would reach out to link up with, connect to, and live in His creation. God shows His love to mankind by reaching down and showing favor and mercy to them. Through this grace, God has called us to be a holy people. Many verses in the Bible attest to that:

> » 2 Timothy 1:9 (NIV): "He has saved us and called us to a holy life -not because of anything we have done but because of his own purpose and grace. This grace was given us in Christ Jesus before the beginning of time."
> » Romans 5:8 (NIV): "God demonstrates His own love for us in this: while we were still sinners, Christ died for us."
> » Romans 5:10 (NIV): "While we were God's enemies, we were reconciled to Him through the death of His Son."
> » Colossians 3:12-15 (BSB): "Therefore, as the elect of God, holy and beloved, clothe yourselves with hearts of compassion, kindness, humility, gentleness, and patience. Bear with one another and forgive any complaint you may have against someone else. Forgive as the Lord forgave you. And over all these virtues put on love, which is the bond of perfect unity. Let the peace of Christ rule in your hearts, for to this you were called as members of one body. And be thankful."

Our God is a covenant-making God. He makes promises and is faithful to see them fulfilled. He promised to show favor and mercy to mankind by sending a redeemer to offer salvation to the lost.

OUR GOD IS A COVENANT-MAKING
GOD. HE MAKES PROMISES AND IS
FAITHFUL TO SEE THEM FULFILLED.

God created the new covenant, also called the covenant of grace, to initiate and carry out His plan for forgiving man's sin, living in man by His Spirit, and giving eternal life. He did this by reaching out to the world and making a pledge between Himself and mankind that ensured that they would be His people, and He would be their God. God would fulfill His promise through His Son, and His Son would be the guarantor and the mediator who would guarantee the faithfulness on both God's part and the believer's part in the pledge. (See Andrew Murray's books *The Two Covenants* and *Jesus, The Mediator of the New Covenant*.)

He (Jesus) is Himself called a covenant (Isaiah 42:6 and 49:8). The union between God and man, which the covenant aims at, was wrought out in Him personally. In Him, the reconciliation between the human and divine was perfectly effected. In Him, His people find the covenant with all its blessings. He is all that God has to give and is the assurance that it is given.

What grace! What amazing grace!

CHAPTER 8
JESUS SENT

"For God so loved the world that He gave His one and only Son, that
whoever believes in him shall not perish but have eternal life."
—JOHN 3:16 (NIV)

G od and mankind were at enmity with each other. But God knew that a relationship founded on covenantal love would be the pathway to bring humankind back to Himself, for covenants are great peace-bearing oaths for those at odds with each other.

"See, a king will reign in righteousness. . . . The fruit
of that righteousness will be peace."
—ISAIAH 32:1 AND 17 (NIV)

God had a plan for mankind even before the beginning of creation, for Jesus was formed to be a part of God's plan. The Nicene Creed says, "He came down for mankind and for our salvation," and John 1:14 (NIV) says, "The Word became flesh and made his dwelling among us. We have seen his glory, the glory of the one and only Son, who came from the Father, full of grace and truth."

God's plan was based on covenantal love. He loved and gave the world His greatest gift:

> "For God so loved the world that He gave His one and only Son, that whoever believes in him shall not perish but have eternal life. [See John 17:3 for what eternal life means.] For God did not send His Son into the world to condemn the world, but to save the world through him." —John 3:16-17 (NIV)

> *"We know how dearly God loves us, because He has given*
> *us the Holy Spirit to fill our hearts with His love."*
> —ROMANS 5:5 (NLT)

GOD'S PLAN IS FOR US TO KNOW HIM AS A COVENANT GOD. THAT TAKES TRUST!

His plan is for us to know Him as a covenant God. That takes trust! God seeks a faithful people to trust in Him. Andrew Murray, in his book *The Master's Indwelling*, says, "Through Christ living in and enabling us, we are able to trust God as Christ trusted Him."[33]

In God's plan, Jesus was sent to fulfill this covenantal promise of peace that I mentioned earlier: a king shall reign in righteousness, the fruit of it will be peace, and it will be evidenced

---

33   Andrew Murray, *The Master's Indwelling* (Scotts Valley, CA: CreateSpace, 2018) 54.

by "quietness and confidence forever" (Isaiah 1:17, NIV). God demonstrated His righteousness by presenting Christ as "a sacrifice of atonement, through the shedding of his blood—to be received by faith. He did this to demonstrate his righteousness" (Romans 3:25, NIV) and "as a bond of friendship and goodwill, as a ground for perfect confidence a covenant has often been of unspeakable value."[34]

God is a covenant God—loving God. He is faithful and keeps His promises.

> *"Jesus is the one who guarantees this better covenant with God."*
> —HEBREWS 7:22 (NIV)

> *"Know therefore that the Lord your God is God, He is the*
> *faithful God, keeping His covenant of love."*
> —DEUTERONOMY 7:9 (NIV)

---

34 Andrew Murray, *The Two Covenants.*

CHAPTER 9

THE NEW COVENANT PROMISE

"The days are coming, declares the Lord, when I will make a new covenant."
—HEBREWS 8:8 (NIV)

I n God's plan, He declared what His covenant for mankind would be:

» Hebrews 8:10 (ESV): "For this is the covenant that I will make with the house of Israel after those days, says the Lord: I will put my laws into their minds, and I will write them on their hearts, and I will be their God, and they shall be my people."

» Ezekiel 36:26 (NIV): "I will give you a new heart and put a new spirit in you; I will remove from you your heart of stone and give you a heart of flesh."

God promised to send a redeemer to bring man back to Himself. This was God's great covenant promise first spoken to the serpent that deceived Eve: "And I will put enmity between thee and the woman, and between thy seed and her seed; it shall bruise thy head, and thou shalt bruise his heel" (Genesis 3:15, KJV).

> GOD PROMISED TO SEND A REDEEMER TO BRING MAN BACK TO HIMSELF.... TO THE BELIEVER, GOD HAS FULFILLED HIS COVENANT THROUGH CHRIST.

To the believer, God has fulfilled His covenant through Christ. First Corinthians 11:25 (NIV) describes how Jesus said, "This cup is the new covenant in My blood." The redeemer is Jesus who came to earth, shed His blood to cleanse us from sin, and was raised to life for our justification. We only get justification by faith.

>> Romans 5:1 (NASB): "Therefore having been justified by faith, we have peace with God through our Lord Jesus Christ."

>> Matthew 26:27 (NIV): "For this is My blood of the covenant, which is poured out for many for the forgiveness of sins.

Matthew Henry's Commentary on Hebrews 12:24 put those thoughts together:

> This covenant is made firm by the blood of Christ sprinkled upon our consciences.... This blood of Christ speaks in behalf of sinners; it pleads not for vengeance, but for

mercy . . . and Christ is the Mediator of the new covenant between God and man, to bring them together in this covenant; to keep them together; to plead with God for us, to plead with us for God.[35]

John Gill's Commentary on 1 Corinthians 11:25, regarding the blood of Christ, said this:

Now this is said to be "in the blood" of Christ; that is, it is ratified and all of its blessings and promises are confirmed by his blood; hence his blood is called "the blood of the everlasting covenant" . . . pardon and righteousness, peace and reconciliation, and entrance into the holiest of all, all come through this blood and are secured by the same . . . to which the faith of the saints is directed . . . to observe, receive and enjoy for themselves.[36]

All of its blessings and promises are confirmed by His blood, "for all of God's promises have been fulfilled in Christ with a resounding 'Yes!'" (2 Corinthians 1:20, NLT).

The new covenant is described as a ministry of righteousness in contrast to the old covenant which is described as a ministry of condemnation. Matthew Henry said the new covenant brings about new life through regeneration:

Our Savior spoke of the necessity and nature of regeneration or the new birth, and at once directed Nicodemus to the source of holiness of the heart. Birth is the beginning of life; to be born again, is to begin to live anew. We must have a new nature, new principles, new affections, new aims.[37]

---

35 Matthew Henry, "Hebrews 12 Bible Commentary," *Christianity*, www.christianity.com/bible/commentary/matthew-henry-complete/hebrews/12.
36 John Gill, "1 Corinthians 11," *Gill's Exposition of the Whole Bible - Bible Commentaries, StudyLight.Org*, www.studylight.org/commentaries/eng/geb/1-corinthians-11.html.
37 Matthew Henry, "John 3 Commentary," *Biblestudytools*, www.biblestudytools.com/commentaries/matthew-henry-concise/john/3.html.

In the new covenant, the Spirit reigns in the heart! Murray's *The Two Covenants* points to 1 Corinthians 2 and 2 Corinthians 3 and explains:

> The New covenant is a ministry of the Spirit. . . . In the New covenant the Holy Spirit is everything. It is the Holy Spirit entering the heart, writing, revealing, impressing upon it God's law and truth, that alone works obedience.[38]

Murray goes on to say that he believes the Spirit's reigning does great things too:

> The heart is the central object of the covenant promise: a heart circumcised to love God fully—a heart where God's love and fear (reverence) has been put, so that it will not depart from Him. (It is this that Jesus assures us under the promise—the oath of God. . . .) God does great things in our hearts. [39]

Matthew Henry sums it up in his Hebrews 12:24 commentary:

> Christ is the Mediator of the New covenant between God and man, to bring them together in this covenant; to keep them together; to plead with God for us, to plead with us for God.[40]

38 Andrew Murray, *The Two Covenants*, 69.
39 Andrew Murray, *The Two Covenants*, 65.
40 Matthew Henry, "Hebrews 12 Bible Commentary."

CHAPTER 10

THE NEW HEART MATTERS

"God's love has been poured out into our hearts through the Holy Spirit."
— ROMANS 5:5 (NIV)

Adam's fall from grace left man with a wicked and evil heart and a separation from God. God declared that He would not only give man a new heart but also place His Spirit in it to maintain that heart.

» Galatians 4:6 (BLB): "God sent forth the Spirit of His Son into our hearts."

» Romans 5:5 (NIV): "God's love has been poured out into our hearts through the Holy Spirit, who has been given to us."

You see? The new heart matters! The Holy Spirit comes to dwell in the believer's heart and gives him the will and power to obey Christ and do the Father's will. The Word tells us to be led by the Spirit and not to fulfill the ways of the flesh. (See Note I:

"The Old Life and the New" on page 113.) You can do this by doing what Paul wrote in Romans 6:13 (NLT), "Give yourselves completely to God, for you were dead, but now you have a new life" with a new heart.

THE NEW HEART MATTERS!

The Holy Spirit reigns in this heart and produces spiritual fruit. (See Note J: "Abiding Fruit" on page 115.) Those fruits include love, joy, peace, patience, kindness, goodness, faithfulness, gentleness, and self-control. The new heart matters, for out of it, the believer treats others as they themselves want to be treated, according to many verses in the Bible, like Matthew 7:12 (ERV), "So whatever you wish that others would do to you, do also to them."

The new heart matters, for out of it, the believer shows kindness and is tenderhearted towards others and forgives those in need of forgiveness.

> *"Be kind to one another, tenderhearted, forgiving one*
> *another, as God in Christ forgave you."*
> — EPHESIANS 4:32 (ESV)

The new heart matters, for the believer confesses before others that Jesus is Lord and that God has saved him/her.

"If you openly declare that Jesus is Lord and believe in your heart
that God raised him from the dead you will be saved."
—ROMANS 10:9 (NLT)

The new heart matters, for God has placed His Spirit there, and love has been spread throughout the heart. This loving heart causes the believer to be patient with and kind to others.

"Love is patient and kind; it is not jealous or conceited or proud."
—1 CORINTHIANS 13:4 (GNT)

The new heart matters! It is where the power of the blood works and blessings are fulfilled: faith, regeneration, redemption, atonement, righteousness, salvation, intercession, and eternal life. This new heart is prepared for Christ to dwell there by His Spirit.

The new heart matters! It is the temple of God—it is where His presence dwells. It is where the work of the Holy Spirit is done. It is the place of faith where one believes. The new heart is the place where God showers His love through Christ Jesus.

The new heart matters! It is where believers find the covenant with all its promises and blessings. Jesus is the mediator of the new covenant. It's all in Jesus—or He is all in all and is Himself called the covenant. He is the one who fulfills all that God has promised the believer, and on the part of the believer he ensures that we are faithful in loving, trusting, and doing God's will. Jesus guarantees that He will fulfill both God's part in the covenant and the believer's part.

JESUS GUARANTEES THAT HE WILL FULFILL BOTH GOD'S PART IN THE COVENANT AND THE BELIEVER'S PART.

The new heart matters, for it is a faith heart—a believing heart. By faith in Christ as the mediator of the new covenant, we have access to the enjoyment of all its promised blessings. All these blessings culminate in one thing: the heart of man being made right to love. (See Note K: "Love in the New Heart" on page 119.)

The new heart matters, for it is in the heart that Christ manifests Himself, and it is there that He and the Father dwell through the Holy Spirit. The new heart is for God's presence. That presence which Adam lost has been regained by the believer through faith in Christ Jesus. With our new heart, we can know and experience unbroken fellowship with God. We have access to His throne of grace and can come boldly to Him in prayer through Christ.

NOTE
REFERENCES

Note A: My Father, A Servant Leader
Note B: What is the Ark of the Covenant?
Note C: The Covenant—A Gift of Love
Note D—Part 1: Marriage and My Upbringing
Note D—Part 2: Marriage and My Experiences
Note D—Part 3: Marriage and the Word
Note E: Just Because of Jesus
Note F—Part 1: All Manner of Wickedness Found
      in Everyday Life
Note F—Part 2: All Manner of Wickedness Found
      in Everyday Life
Note G: The Covenant of Grace
Note H: Born Again
Note I: The Old Life and the New
Note J: Abiding Fruit
Note K: Love in the New Heart

MY FATHER, A SERVANT LEADER

LESSONS OF DADDY'S LIFE RETAIN THEIR IMPACT TODAY

by Lorraine K. Flood—January 30, 2003

"Service with a Smile!" The sign hung glaringly at the front of my father's shop on Chapel Street. My father, Russell V. Kelley, Sr., was among those who owned a business in the black community after World War II. The shop was a cleaners and a place where he did alterations. In my mind's eye, I still see the fast movement of his feet as they seesawed back and forth on the lattice-like treadle and hear the whirring hum of his old sewing machine as he put cuffs on a customer's pants.

Daddy believed in doing the right thing: treating others fairly, helping those in need, and telling the truth. He did not put up with foolishness from anyone. Once, on our way home from a Sunday drive in the country, my dad discovered chirping biddies undercover in the back seat of our car. With a whirlwind of a turn, he headed back to the scene of the crime, lecturing us about acting foolish. Taking biddies from his friend's yard, without asking, was not the right thing to do. He reminded my brothers that they had embarrassed our family.

In the work world, my father was known to speak up for those who dared not. Standard Cleaners provided services to many of the families in Huntersville and the surrounding neighborhoods from the late 40s to the early 60s. Like his grandfather, who also owned a business during the early 20s—a community convenience store at the corner of Bottimore and Hull Streets in what is now West Ghent—my daddy worked full-time at the Norfolk Naval Yard in Portsmouth. He and his siblings worked in their grandfather's shop after school, just as my siblings and I worked in my father's shop.

For us, going to the shop was a chore. When the customers brought in clothes to be cleaned, we wrote out a carbon-copy ticket. Next, we would tag the clothes by writing the ticket number on the pronged metal tag and attaching the tags to the garments in two places. Then, we would record the name, ticket number, items, and cost in a ledger. The clothes were then separated into various categories, ready for the driver from the main plant.

When the driver returned the clothes, we would match them against the ledger. As customers picked up their clothes, the process ended with "Thank you, and have a nice evening."

We went to the shop daily. Daddy would relieve us after going home for dinner. At about 6 o'clock, he would come to the shop, and at 8:30 p.m., get his hat, turn the sign to "Closed," and lock up for the night.

The most remarkable thing about my father was how he managed his time so he could be involved in the community. For well over thirty years, he was an active leader in the community. At church, he was a deacon and a clerk. On the national level, he was a leader in the Lott Carey Laymen League, a mission-minded group of men.

In education, during the 50s, he was president of the PTA at John T. West Elementary School and, later, at Booker T. Washington High School.

In the community, my father served as president of the Huntersville Model City Commission from 1971-1975. He served as treasurer of the Norfolk Citizen Participation Council, Inc., from 1974 to 1983. He had been the first vice president of the Norfolk Inner-City Federal Credit Union and past president of the Olde Huntersville Civic League.

As I grew up in Huntersville, the community was woven together with single-family homes, brick apartments, churches, libraries, and many family-owned businesses, including corner markets, barber shops, beauty shops, a gas station, drug stores, ice cream stores, shoe shops, a confectionary store, fish markets, and a laundromat. Together, they gave our community an appearance of being self-sustaining.

Though this was the era of segregation, people in our community lived together in close harmony. People were neighborly. They borrowed sugar. They talked over their fences. They sat on their porches while children skipped hopscotch, jumped rope, and played baseball. In the evening, men returned home from work with lunch pails in hand. Children went to schools in their neighborhoods: John T. West, Laura E. Titus, Dunbar, J.C. Price, Jacox Jr. High, Ruffner Jr. High, and Booker T. Washington High School.

There were annual events that unified the community. On Memorial Day, for instance, families and friends met at Calvary Cemetery, talking and laughing as they dressed the gravesites of their loved ones with freshly cut flowers.

Another big event was the Thanksgiving Eve football game between the famous rivals: Booker T. and Norcom of Portsmouth. The half-time performance was a showdown between the schools' bands.

Ask anyone from the community what was synonymous with the Fourth of July, and they probably would say Daddy Grace's parade. High-stepping majorettes, loudly playing drummers, swaying ladies, and lively bands playing upbeat music sent a festive mood throughout the community.

I was twelve years old when I started going to the shop. I worked there through my sophomore year of college in 1962. I think the best lesson for me was acquiring a great sense of identity, which promotes confidence and a healthy sense of boldness—two traits that I believe drive leaders to action.

That's what these leadership qualities have done for my siblings and me. We all have given back to the community by being devoted to the church, raising loving families, excelling as educators, serving in the military, owning a law firm, working in the corporate world, and serving in politics. After all, life comes from the father, and our father is in us.

"My Father, a Servant-Leader" is the sign that hangs tenderly on the wall of my memory. He gave his life to the community so that others might live a quality life. What a legacy to my family! What a gift to the community!

WHAT IS THE ARK OF THE COVENANT?

The ark of the covenant was an object used for worship by the ancient Israelites. Moses's instructions regarding how it should be built and used can be found in Exodus 25:10-22. The following explanation of its significance is from Got Questions Ministries and can be found, along with other pertinent information, on the ministry's website.[41]

> God made a covenant (a conditional covenant) with the children of Israel through His servant Moses. He promised good to them and their children for generations if they obeyed Him and His laws; but He always warned of despair, punishment, and dispersion if they were to disobey. As a sign of His covenant He had the Israelites make a box according to His own design, in which to place the stone tablets containing the Ten Commandments. This box, or chest, was called an "ark" and was made of acacia wood overlaid with gold. The Ark was to be housed in the inner sanctum of the tabernacle

---

41 "What Is the Ark of the Covenant?" GotQuestions.Org, 25 June 2010, www.gotquestions.org/ark-of-the-covenant.html.

in the desert and eventually in the Temple when it was built in Jerusalem. This chest is known as the Ark of the covenant.

The real significance of the Ark of the covenant was what took place involving the lid of the box, known as the "Mercy Seat." The term 'mercy seat' comes from a Hebrew word meaning "to cover, placate, appease, cleanse, cancel or make atonement for." It was here that the high priest, only once a year (Leviticus 16), entered the Holy of Holies where the Ark was kept and atoned for his sins and the sins of the Israelites. The priest sprinkled blood of a sacrificed animal onto the Mercy Seat to appease the wrath and anger of God for past sins committed. This was the only place in the world where this atonement could take place.

The Mercy Seat on the Ark was a symbolic foreshadowing of the ultimate sacrifice for all sin—the blood of Christ shed on the cross for the remission of sins. The Apostle Paul, a former Pharisee and one familiar with the Old Testament, knew this concept quite well when he wrote about Christ being our covering for sin in Romans 3:24-25: "...and are justified by his grace as a gift, through the redemption that is in Christ Jesus, whom God put forward as a propitiation by his blood, to be received by faith." Just as there was only one place for atonement of sins in the Old Testament—the Mercy Seat of the Ark of the covenant—so there is also only one place for atonement in the New Testament and current times—the cross of Jesus Christ. As Christians, we no longer look to the Ark but to the Lord Jesus Himself as the propitiation and atonement for our sins.

NOTE C

THE COVENANT— A GIFT OF LOVE

by Lorraine K. Flood*—February 14, 2017

Personal Note: My name changed to Lorraine K. Bullock in September 2018.

Peace can be established when two or more parties come together in a bonding relationship. This is what a covenant does; it creates a bond of relationships. Our God is a covenant God who desires fellowship with mankind. He loves us with a love that's forever, a love that never fails. In Psalm 89:28 (NIV), the writer points to this everlasting love, "I will maintain my love to him forever, and my covenant with him will never fail."

I want to know more about God's covenant than what's written about throughout the Bible. Let me share with you the reason why. One evening, about three years ago, I was drawn to my study to spend a quiet time before the Lord. While on my knees, in complete quietness, I began to sense the word "covenant" in my spirit. Just a few years earlier, my sister and two close friends and I had participated in a book talk discussion using Chuck Swindoll's book, *David*.[42] We read and talked about the ark of the covenant and understood that the different items in the ark and the ark itself had a deeper spiritual meaning. Other than that, I had not paid much attention to the word covenant. Before leaving my study, I knew that the Holy Spirit was guiding me on a promised land journey—the study of the covenant.

So, what is a covenant? At its basic level, according to Theopedia, a covenant is defined simply as "a binding agreement or compact between two or more parties; in legal terms, it is a formal sealed agreement or contract."[43]

In Mark Jones's article "What Is a Covenant?" he writes, "In divine covenants, God sovereignly establishes the relationship with His creatures . . . and God binds Himself by His own oath to keep His promises."[44] The sovereignty of God, found in Theopedia, is "the biblical teaching that all things are under God's rule and control. . . ."[45]

In Stephen Pimentel's work, "The Master Key: Pope Benedict XVI's Theology of Covenant," he begins by explaining the word covenant: "In the biblical conception, a covenant is not a contract or mutual agreement between God and man, but an unsought gift of God to man."[46]

---

42 Charles R. Swindoll, *David: A Man of Passion & Destiny*.
43 "Covenant," *Theopedia.Com*, www.theopedia.com/covenant.
44 Mark Jones "What Is a Covenant?" *Ligonier Ministries*, 24 Apr. 2014, www.ligonier.org/learn/articles/what-covenant.
45 "Sovereignty of God," *Theopedia.Com*, https://www.theopedia.com/sovereignty-of-god.
46 Stephen Pimentel, "The Master Key: Pope Benedict XVI's Theology of Covenant," *Catholic Culture*, www.catholicculture.org/culture/library/view.cfm?recnum=7878.

Pimentel quotes Joseph Cardinal Ratzinger, now Pope Benedict XVI, "The covenant then is not a pact built on reciprocity, but rather a gift, a creative act of God's love."[47] Moses called what God had committed to us a covenant of love. In Psalm 89:28 (NIV), the writer declared that God is mighty and faithful and "will maintain my love to him forever, and my covenant with him will never fail."

God is love. Love is His nature. Man, because of Adam's sin, is selfish and full of pride. Man's heart is the big problem. His heart is deceitful and full of sin. It locks out love and God's life, as well as all other spiritual blessings. Man's nature is that of the "self." He believes that he can live by his own self-effort, self-confidence, and self-improvement. Depending on self in our spiritual lives never works, for man's unregenerate heart fights against God. Man's heart had to be changed. Sin had to be forgiven.

God had a plan to remove man's sin. He initiated a plan of love—a covenant. This covenant would bring God and His people together in a binding relationship. God promised that He would give His people a new heart and put the right spirit in them. God prepared a blood sacrifice to confirm His covenant. God sent His Son.

Jesus was born, lived on earth as a man, died on the cross for our sins, and was buried in a tomb with a rolling stone covering the entrance. God resurrected Jesus to life, Jesus met with his believers, and then He ascended into heaven and went to the right hand of the Father where he was given the Holy Spirit. Jesus sent the Spirit into the hearts of the believers. Romans 5:5 (NIV) says, "God's love has been poured out into our hearts through

---

47   Stephen Pimentel, "The Master Key: Pope Benedict XVI's Theology of Covenant."

the Holy Spirit who has been given to us." God promised that He would change our heart and put the right spirit in us, like in Romans 10:10 (NIV): "For it is with your heart that you believe and are justified."

God is a covenant God. It is a gift of love and can be seen at the Last Supper (Matthew 26:28, BSB) where Jesus confirmed that "My blood is the covenant" between God and His people. It is poured out as a sacrifice to forgive the sins of many. God has "cut" a covenant with us through Jesus.

Another inexpressible gift of love can be seen in Romans 5:8 (ESV): "But God shows His love for us in that while we were still sinners, Christ died for us." His blood has cleansed our hearts from sin and replaced it with Jesus Christ's righteousness, according to 1 Corinthians 1:30 (NLT):

> God has united you with Christ Jesus. For our benefit, God made him to be wisdom itself. Christ made us right with God; he made us pure and holy, and he freed us from sin.

God is love (1 John 4:16), and "This is love; not that we loved God, but that He loved us and sent His Son as an atoning sacrifice for our sins" (1 John 4:10, NIV). I mentioned in chapter 1 that Charles Spurgeon expounded on this in his sermon titled "Love": "We love Him because He first loved us and in that first love there is the pledge and promise that He will love us even to the end."[48]

The covenant is about man's heart being made right. God and Jesus Christ come to dwell in the heart of the believer through the Holy Spirit. God's love never fails. (See 1 Corinthians 13:8).

That's God's promise. That's God's covenant. THAT'S GOD'S GIFT OF LOVE!

---

48 Charles Spurgeon, "Love."

MARRIAGE AND MY UPBRINGING

Aleyshia, if you know me, then you must know that I view marriage from a Christian perspective. There are three factors that have shaped my beliefs regarding marriage: my upbringing, personal experiences, and the Word.

First, let me tell you about growing up during the 1940s and the 1950s. We had a tight-knit family and lived in a tight-knit community. The majority of our adult family members were married. The majority of the households in our neighborhood included married couples with children. I grew up going to church. All around me at church were families that included moms and dads that were married. The culture that I grew up in was made up of families which included married couples with children. I was shaped by my environment and its people, places, and things.

When I was finishing the twelfth grade, one of my friends interviewed me and asked me what I was looking forward to in the future. I responded, "I want a family, and I want to make my husband happy." I was seventeen at that time and had that vision. Last year, your granddaddy and I celebrated fifty years of marriage. I will point you to a letter that I wrote to the editor of *The Virginian-Pilot* in 2007 titled "7-7-7-7-7-7-7." It points to how we were able to overcome the "devil" of miscommunication by following the advice found in Matthew 18:22. I believe what you find there is the key to relationships: forgiveness.

NOTE D—PART 2

MARRIAGE AND MY EXPERIENCES

Now, forgiveness is at the heart of Christianity. You know that we come into the saving grace of Jesus through forgiveness. When things are reconciled, we can then fellowship with the Father. Well, it works the same way in marriage. When the couple experiences challenges, hurts, arguments, and on and on and on . . . one forgives the other. The forgiveness is received, and then, they make up. Things are reconciled, and you move on.

I believe that forgiveness is a spiritual action and characteristic right from the heart of the Father, and we can know it only through Jesus. The reason I say it's only from Jesus is because as Christians, we die to ourselves that Jesus might live His life in and through us. Otherwise, we live our own selfish lives. Forgiveness is hardly in our thoughts; therefore, we hardly forgive and truly make up. Long-lasting marriages are built on the premise of "forgiveness and making-up." Making up is hard to do without its partner, forgiveness, which is Jesus. Jesus is forgiveness, and

He, Forgiveness, lives in us. With that said, we can forgive any and everything that's done against us. I believe this. I know this.

MARRIAGE AND THE WORD

There are familiar verses in the Word (the Bible) that most people know and often use when referring to family matters:

» Proverbs 22:6 (ESV): "Train up a child in the way he should go. . . ."

» Ephesians 5:25 (NIV): "Husbands, love your wives, just as Christ loved the church."

» Ephesians 6:1 (BSB:)"Children obey your parents. . . ."

But the word that has influenced me most regarding the family matter of marriage is found in Malachi 2:15. It points to the purpose of marriage. The Message says,

> "God, not you, made marriage. His Spirit inhabits even the smallest details of marriage. And what does He want from marriage?"

The NIV (I like this version) says,

> "Has not the Lord made them one? In flesh and spirit they are His. And why one? Because He was seeking godly offspring. So guard yourself in your spirit."

Aleyshia, I believe that marriage is a spiritual partnership. When there is intimacy—oneness—so much is poured into each other. There is giving and receiving. There is peace and joy. There is celebration and jubilation. There are soft voices and sensual moans, and godly fruit—godly offspring—are born.

The Word declares that marriage is a mystery. Only God can reveal the truth of that mystery.

To the praise of His glory!

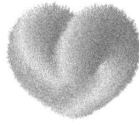

JUST BECAUSE OF JESUS

MY DECLARATIONS

by Lorraine K. Bullock—September 5, 2022

» God sent His Son to free us from our sin nature by taking away our sins. (Colossians 2:13-14)
» All have sinned. (Romans 3:23)
» God declares believers not guilty because of their faith in Jesus. (Romans 3:20-24)
» Jesus's light revealed my sinful ways. (2 Corinthians 4:6)
» Because of Jesus, God led me to repent and turn away from sin. (1 John 1:9)
» Because of Jesus Christ, God freely accepts me and sets me free from sin. (Romans 3:24)
» And now, I have a new obedient heart (with a desire to be faithful) because of Jesus. (Ezekiel 36:26)

» I've been saved by grace through faith (it is the gift of God) because of Jesus. (Ephesians 2:8)

» Because of Jesus, I have love in my heart put there by His Spirit. (Romans 5:5)

» I am born again. (1 Peter 1:3 and 23)

» God accepts sinners because they have faith in Jesus. (Romans 4:5)

» I am redeemed (sacrificial blood was the price paid for my sin) because of Jesus. (Ephesians 1:7)

» But now I am free from the power of sin because of Jesus. (Romans 6:20-23)

» I am reconciled: brought back to the Father because of Jesus. (2 Corinthians 5:18-21)

» I am a new creation. (2 Corinthians 5:17)

» I have a brand-new nature created by Jesus Christ. (Colossians 3:9-10)

» The life that I now live, I live by faith in Christ Jesus. (Galatians 2:20)

» I am sealed with the promised Holy Spirit because of Jesus. (Ephesians 1:13-14)

» Because of Jesus, I am righteous: right with God. (2 Corinthians 5:18-21)

» Because of Jesus, I've been led to the obedience that comes from faith in Him. (Romans 16:26)

» I am ensured power to maintain obedience because of Jesus. (Ezekiel 36:27)

» The Holy Spirit reigns in my heart because of Jesus. (2 Corinthians 3:3, 6, 17)

» I share in God's divine nature because of Jesus. (1 Peter 1:3-5)

» Because of Jesus, I live by God's power. This is the kingdom of God. (1 Corinthians 4:20)

» Because of Jesus, I have power over my sinful nature. (2 Corinthians 12:9)

» I believe in and receive God's wonderful promises because of Jesus. (2 Peter 1:3-5)

» All God's promises are fulfilled and confirmed because of Jesus. (2 Corinthians 1:20)

» Because of Jesus, I can apply the benefits of these promises to my life. (2 Peter 1:3-5)

» My testimony to others when something is misplaced is "There is nothing lost in the Spirit!"

» It's a great promise of Jesus. (Luke 8:17 and Mark 4:22)

» Because of Jesus, blessings chase after me. (Proverbs 13:21)

» Because of the stripes of Jesus, I am healed. (Isaiah 53:4-5)

» I enter God's presence with thanksgiving because of Jesus. (Psalm 95:2)

» Because of Jesus, my earnest prayer has great power and wonderful results. (James 5:16)

» Just because of Jesus, I have eternal life! (John 3:16)

Amen!

ALL MANNER OF WICKEDNESS FOUND IN EVERYDAY LIFE

by Lorraine K. Bullock—October 10, 2020

Well, over seventy-five years ago, I grew up and lived in a neighborly black community. It was a time of cultural segregation where black and white races were separated in various ways. Neighborhoods were segregated. Churches were segregated. Schools were segregated.

During the 50s, Blacks were not allowed to eat at lunch counters in department stores, and white-owned restaurants would not seat Blacks for services. Whites and Blacks could neither drink out of the same water fountains nor use the same restrooms. Signs would be placed on the restroom doors and on the water fountains that read "Whites Only" and "For Coloreds Only."

Racism inundated our everyday lives. Civil rights was the theme of that time. In 1955, Rosa Parks helped to bring attention to seating on public transportation in Montgomery, Alabama. Blacks were ordered to take the back seats on the bus if white people wanted the ones in front, but she sat on a seat in the front and refused to give it up to a white man. Black leaders in the community, led by Martin Luther King Jr., were inspired to action and organized the Montgomery Bus Boycott which eventually led to the ruling by the US Supreme Court that bus segregation was unconstitutional. This was one way to address racism in the country.

It is now 2020, and structural racism still exists in a systematic manner. In a 2018 case study by Connor Maxwell and Danyelle Solomon, the Aspen Institute stated that "Structural racism is defined as a system of public policies, institutional practices, cultural representations and other norms that work in reinforcing ways to perpetuate racial inequality."[49] During today's time, many are concerned and working towards ensuring that their community is a safe place in which to live, work, and move about. Some places are not safe, for there are communities plagued with gangs and drugs, shootings and killings, and rape and sex trafficking—sometimes even involving children.

There are home environments that are toxic because of the abusive behaviors between husbands and wives and, many times, between parents and their children. American families are torn apart by the many divorces that occur annually. According to the law offices of GillespieShields, there are 2,419,196 divorces

---

49 *Glossary for Understanding the Dismantling Structural Racism/Promoting ...*, www.aspeninstitute.org/wp-content/uploads/files/content/docs/rcc/RCC-Structural-Racism-Glossary.pdf.

per year.[50] Families are also impacted in many other ways: out-of-wedlock births, homelessness, mental health issues, and incarcerations—especially among black men. In the 2016 article "The Color of Justice: Racial and Ethnic Disparity in State Prisons" by Dr. Ashley Nellis, it was reported that "African Americans are incarcerated in state prisons across the country at more than 5 times the rate of whites."[51] This incarceration issue seems to point to bias against Blacks which is morally wrong and proceeds from a deceitful heart.

In the commentary *Barnes' Notes on the Bible*, for Matthew 15:10-20, you'll find the following words, "Christ . . . states what does defile the man."[52] That is what makes the man unclean. Jesus said, "But the words you speak come from the heart, and that's what defiles you" (Matthew 15:18, NLT). (Defiles—Pollutes, corrupts or renders sinful.[53]) *Gill's Exposition of the Entire Bible* includes the following: "It is sin, and that only, which takes its rise from the heart, lies in thought, and is either expressed by the mouth or performed by some outward action which defiles the man."[54]

> » Dana had agreed to make a presentation at church on Sunday. She arrived during the time the pastor was speaking to the congregation. When the pastor noticed her walking down the aisle, he said, "Oh, here is

50 "Family Law Attorney in Phoenix & Mesa: Specialists in Probate Law & Estate Planning, Civil, Employment, Immigration, Appellate & Criminal Law," *GillespieShields*, 13 May 2023, gillespieshields.com/.
51 Ashley Nellis, "The Color of Justice: Racial and Ethnic Disparity in State Prisons," *The Sentencing Project*, 16 Dec. 2022, www.sentencingproject.org/reports/the-color-of-justice-racial-and-ethnic-disparity-in-state-prisons-the-sentencing-project/.
52 "Matthew 15 - Barnes' Notes on the Whole Bible - Bible Commentaries," *StudyLight.Org*, www.studylight.org/commentaries/eng/bnb/matthew-15.html.
53 "Matthew 15 - Barnes' Notes on the Whole Bible - Bible Commentaries."
54 John Gill, "Matthew 15:11 - Bible Verse Meaning and Commentary," *Biblestudytools.Com*, www.biblestudytools.com/commentaries/gills-exposition-of-the-bible/matthew-15-11.html#:~:text=It%20is%20sin%2C%20and%20that,in%20the%20sight%20of%20God.

Dana—late as usual." These insulting words came from his heart and expressed itself as a sinful act.

» When the usher passed the offering plate, the couple pretended to put money in as the plate passed by them. What hypocrisy! It proceeds from the heart.

» Claire is married. She saw an old boyfriend at Hawkin's Club. They greeted each other in a jovial manner. The couple talked about old times. He asked to see her again, and she agreed. They met in a private cozy place and became sexually intimate. (See Mark 7:21 (ESV): "For from within, out of the heart of man, come evil thoughts, sexual immorality.")

A. B. Simpson, nineteenth-century founder of the Christian Missionary Alliance, said the following in his book *Days of Heaven Upon Earth*:

> The flesh [human nature] is incurably bad. "It is not subject to the law of God, neither, indeed, can be." It never can be any better. It is no use trying to improve the flesh. You may educate it all you please. You may train it by the most approved methods, you may set before it the brightest examples, you may pipe to it or mourn to it, treat it with encouragement or severity; its nature will always be incorrigibly the same. The only remedy for human nature is to destroy it, and receive instead the divine nature. God does not improve man. He crucifies the natural life with Christ, and creates the new man in Christ Jesus. [55]

55 A. B. Simpson, *Days of Heaven Upon Earth: A Year Book of Scripture Texts and Living Truths* (Brooklyn, NY: Christian Alliance Pub. Co., 1897).

ALL MANNER OF WICKEDNESS FOUND IN EVERYDAY LIFE

In the title of this writing, the word "wickedness" is expressed. It is defined at Lexico.com as "the quality of being evil or morally wrong." Find listed below what it means to be wicked as described in the *Oxford Dictionary*:

Godly Behavior: Truth

GOSSIP	TATTLE	RUMORS
Whispers	Tales	Idle talk
Scandal	Hearsay	Malicious
Smear campaign	Dirt	Mud-slinging

Godly Behavior: Faithfulness

ADULTERY	UNFAITHFUL-NESS	INFIDELITY
Disloyalty	Extramarital sex	Affair
Cheating	Two-timing	Fooling around
Playing the field	Hanky panky	Fornication

Godly Behavior: Praise/Worship

WITCH	WIZARD	SORCERER
Magician	Diviner	Occultist
Voodooist	Black Magic	Astrology

Godly Behavior: Temperance

INDECENCY	LEWDNESS	LUSTFULNESS
Promiscuity	Indecency	Licentiousness

Godly Behavior: Righteousness

EVIL	THEFT	EVIL-DOING
Sin	Sinfulness	Iniquity
Vileness	Foulness	Baseness
Badness	Wrong	Wrongdoing

THE COVENANT OF GRACE

"Sin shall not have dominion over you: for ye are
not under the law, but under grace."
—ROMANS 6:14 (KJV)

The following is an excerpt from Andrew Murray's *The Two Covenants*:

> The words, covenant of grace, though not found in Scripture, are the correct expression of the truth it abundantly teaches, that the contrast between the two covenants is none other than that of law and grace. Of the New covenant, grace is the great characteristic: "The law came in, that the offence might abound; but where sin abounded, grace did abound more exceedingly." It is to bring the Romans away entirely from under the Old covenant, and to teach them their place in the New, that Paul writes: "Ye are not under the law, but under grace." And he assures them that if they believe this, and live in it, their experience would confirm God's promise: " Sin shall not have dominion over you." What the law could not do—give deliverance from the power of sin

over us—grace would effect. The New covenant was entirely a covenant of grace. In the wonderful grace of God it had its origin; it was meant to be a manifestation of the riches and the glory of that grace; of grace, and by grace working in us, all its promises can be fulfilled and experienced.

The word grace is used in two senses. It is first the gracious disposition in God which moves Him to love us freely without our merit, and to bestow all His blessings upon us. Then it also means that power through which this grace does its work in us. The redeeming work of Christ, and the righteousness He won for us, equally with the work of the Spirit in us, as the power of the new life, are spoken of as Grace. It includes all that Christ has done and still does, all He has and gives, all He is for us and in us. John says, "We beheld His glory, the glory of the Only Begotten of the Father, full of grace and truth." "The law was given by Moses, grace and truth came by Jesus Christ." "And of His fulness have all we received, and grace for grace." What the law demands, grace supplies.

BORN AGAIN

"There was a man of the Pharisees, named Nicodemus, a ruler of the Jews."
—JOHN 3:1 (KJV)

The following is an excerpt from *Matthew Henry's Commentary* on John 3:21, which can be found at BibleStudyTools.com:

> Nicodemus was afraid, or ashamed to be seen with Christ, therefore came in the night. When religion is out of fashion, there are many Nicodemites. But though he came by night, Jesus bid him welcome, and hereby taught us to encourage good beginnings, although weak. And though now he came by night, yet afterward he owned Christ publicly. He did not talk with Christ about state affairs, though he was a ruler, but about the concerns of his own soul and its salvation, and went at once to them. Our Savior spoke of the necessity and nature of regeneration or the new birth, and at once directed Nicodemus to the source of holiness of the heart. Birth is the beginning of life; to be born again, is to begin to live anew, as those who have lived much amiss, or to little purpose. We must have a new nature, new principles, new affections, new aims. By our first birth we were corrupt, shapen in sin; therefore we must be made new creatures.

No stronger expression could have been chosen to signify a great and most remarkable change of state and character.

We must be entirely different from what we were before, as that which begins to be at any time, is not, and cannot be the same with that which was before. This new birth is from heaven, ch. 1:13, and its tendency is to heaven. It is a great change made in the heart of a sinner, by the power of the Holy Spirit. It means that something is done in us, and for us, which we cannot do for ourselves. Something is wrong, whereby such a life begins as shall last forever. We cannot otherwise expect any benefit by Christ; it is necessary to our happiness here and hereafter. What Christ speak, Nicodemus misunderstood, as if there had been no other way of regenerating and new-molding an immortal soul, than by new-framing the body.

But he acknowledged his ignorance, which shows a desire to be better informed. It is then further explained by the Lord Jesus. He shows the Author of this blessed change. It is not wrought by any wisdom or power of our own, but by the power of the blessed Spirit. We are shapen in iniquity, which makes it necessary that our nature be changed. We are not to marvel at this; for, when we consider the holiness of God, the depravity of our nature, and the happiness set before us, we shall not think it strange that so much stress is laid upon this. The regenerating work of the Holy Spirit is compared to water. It is also probable that Christ had reference to the ordinance of baptism. Not that all those, and those only, that are baptized, are saved; but without that new birth which is wrought by the Spirit, and signified by baptism, none shall be subjects of the kingdom of heaven.

The same word signifies both the wind and the Spirit. The wind bloweth where it listeth for us; God directs it. The Spirit sends his influences where, and when, on whom, and in what measure and degree, he pleases. Though the causes are hidden, the effects are plain, when the soul is brought to mourn for sin, and to breathe after Christ. Christ's stating of the doctrine and the necessity of regeneration, it should seem, made it not clearer to Nicodemus. Thus the things of the Spirit of God are foolishness to the natural man. Many think that cannot be proved, which they cannot believe. Christ's discourse of gospel truths, ver. 11-13, shows the folly of those who make these things strange unto them; and it recommends us to search them out. Jesus Christ is every way able to reveal the will of God to us; for he came down from heaven, and yet is in heaven. We have here a notice of Christ's two distinct natures in one person, so that while he is the Son of man, yet he is in heaven. God is the "HE THAT IS," and heaven is the dwelling-place of his holiness.[56]

56 Matthew Henry, "John 3 Commentary," *Biblestudytools.com*, www.biblestudytools.com/commentaries/matthew-henry-concise/john/3.html.

THE OLD LIFE AND THE NEW

"You must put to death, then, the earthly desires at work in you, such as sexual immorality, indecency, lust, evil passions, and greed (for greed is a form of idolatry). Because of such things God's anger will come upon those who do not obey him. At one time you yourselves used to live according to such desires, when your life was dominated by them.

But now you must get rid of all these things: anger, passion, and hateful feelings. No insults or obscene talk must ever come from your lips. Do not lie to one another, for you have put off the old self with its habits and have put on the new self. This is the new being which God, its Creator, is constantly renewing in his own image, in order to bring you to a full knowledge of himself. As a result, there is no longer any distinction between Gentiles and Jews, circumcised and uncircumcised, barbarians, savages, slaves, and free, but Christ is all, Christ is in all.

You are the people of God; he loved you and chose you for his own. So then, you must clothe yourselves with compassion, kindness, humility, gentleness, and patience. Be tolerant with one another and forgive one another whenever any of you has a complaint against someone else. You must forgive one another just as the Lord has forgiven you. And to all these qualities add love, which binds all things together in perfect unity. The peace that Christ gives is to guide you in the decisions you make; for it is to this peace that God has called you together in the one body. And be thankful. Christ's message in all its richness must live in your hearts. Teach and instruct one another with all wisdom. Sing psalms, hymns, and sacred songs; sing to God with thanksgiving in your hearts. Everything you do or say, then, should be done in the name of the Lord Jesus, as you give thanks through him to God the Father."

—COLOSSIANS 3:5-17 (GNT)

ABIDING FRUIT

*"I chose you, and appointed you, that ye should go and
bear fruit, and that your fruit should abide."*
—JOHN 15:16 (NKJV)

The following is an excerpt of *The True Vine: Meditations for a
Month* on John 15:1-16 by Andrew Murray:

> There are some fruits that will not keep. One sort of pears
> or apples must be used at once; another sort can be kept
> over till next year. So there is in Christian work some fruit
> that does not last. There may be much that pleases and
> edifies, and yet there is no permanent impression made on
> the power of the world or the state of the Church. On the
> other hand, there is work that leaves its mark for generations
> or for eternity. In it the power of God makes itself lastingly
> felt. It is the fruit of which Paul speaks when he describes the
> two styles of ministry: "My preaching was not in persuasive
> words of wisdom, but in demonstrations of the Spirit and
> of power; that your faith should not stand in the wisdom of
> men, but in the power of God." The more of man with his
> wisdom and power, the less of stability; the more of God's
> Spirit, the more of a faith standing in God's power.

Fruit reveals the nature of the tree from which it comes. What is the secret of bearing fruit that abides? The answer is simple. It is as our life abides in Christ, as we abide in Him, that the fruit we bear will abide. The more we allow all that is of human will and effort to be cut down short and cleansed away by the divine Husbandman, the more intensely our being withdraws itself from the outward that God may work in us by His Spirit; that is, the more wholly we abide in Christ, the more will our fruit abide.

What a blessed thought! He chose you, and appointed you to bear fruit, and that your fruit should abide. He never meant one of His branches to bring forth fruit that should not abide.

The deeper I enter into the purpose of this His electing grace, the surer my confidence will become that I can bring forth fruit to eternal life, for myself and others. The deeper I enter into this purpose of His electing love, the more I will realize what the link is between the purpose from eternity, and the fruit to eternity: the abiding in Him. The purpose is His, He will carry it out; the fruit is His, He will bring it forth; the abiding is His, He will maintain it.

Let everyone who professes to be a Christian worker, pause. Ask whether you are leaving your mark for eternity on those around you. It is not your preaching or teaching, your strength of will or power to influence, that will secure this. All depends on having your life full of God and His power. And that again depends upon your living the truly branchlike life of abiding —very close and unbroken fellowship with Christ. It is the branch, that abides in Him, that brings forth much fruit, fruit that will abide.

Blessed Lord, reveal to my soul, I pray Thee, that Thou hast chosen me to bear much fruit. Let this be my confidence, that Thy purpose can be realized .-Thou didst choose me. Let this be my power to forsake everything and give myself to Thee. Thou wilt Thyself perfect what Thou hast begun.

Draw me so to dwell in the love and the certainty of that eternal purpose, that the power of eternity may possess me, and the fruit I bear may abide. That ye may bear fruit. O my heavenly Vine, it is beginning to dawn upon my soul that fruit, more fruit—much fruit —abiding fruit is the one thing Thou hast to give me, and the one thing as branch I have to give Thee! Here I am. Blessed Lord, work out Thy purpose in me; let me bear much fruit, abiding fruit, to thy glory.[57]

---

57 Andrew Murray, *The True Vine* (Chicago, IL: Moody Publishers, 2007) 73

LOVE IN THE NEW HEART

1 Corinthians 13:1-7

God is love. He uses the virtue of love through the Holy Spirit to bind Himself together with believers and believers with Himself. He does the work. It's His grace. God's Word tells us: "For this is how God loved the world: He gave his one and only Son" (John 3:16, NLT).

Based on His love, God promised His chosen people who lived in evil and wicked ways that He would give them a new heart and put a new spirit in them. He did this by having His Holy Spirit spread love throughout the hearts of those who believed in Him. Those who believe receive a new heart where God dwells by His Spirit, and love permeates throughout their lives. This new nature of the believer has divine power and is capable of displaying love to God and to others.

This love for others growing out of God's love for us:

[E]ndures with patience and serenity, love is kind and thoughtful, and is not jealous or envious; love does not brag and is not proud or arrogant. It is not rude; it is not self-seeking; it is not provoked [nor overly sensitive and easily angered]; it does not take into account a wrong endured. It does not rejoice at injustice but rejoices with the truth [when right and truth prevail]. Love bears all things [regardless of what comes], believes all things [looking for the best in each one], hopes all things [remaining steadfast during difficult times], endures all things [without weakening]. —1 Corinthians 13:4-7 (AMP)

THE GIFT OF LOVE BUNDLED TOGETHER IN FAMILY

A COVENANT PROMISE TO THE FAMILY

This book was inspired by a quiet encounter with the Lord while in prayer when I sensed God's voice speaking the word "covenant" in my heart and knew that God by His Spirit was leading me on a promise-land journey to find out the biblical meaning of "covenant" and to know about God as a Covenant God. It is merged with a section entitled "The Gift of Love: Bundled Together in Family" from the author's view as a widow, a mother, a grandmother, and a wife.

GROWING UP; MARRIAGE; CONVERSION

1) Growing Up

This prologue is the story of the early years of my life where I grew up and a description of the community where I lived. It tells about my parents and their involvement at home, work, at church and other involvements in the community.

2) Marriage

My late husband and I were married for 52 years. We married in 1963 and had five children. He died unexpectedly in early April 2016 after having back surgery. He was known for always saying, "Have I told U I Love You Today?" To which many would respond, "You got me." He would then say, "Pass it on!"

3) Conversion

I was baptized when I was 9 years old and experienced my conversion 20 years later. I was 29 years old. On a night in October 1971, I was looking at a Christian program on television where many of the guests had shared their conversion experience. I began to desire and want such an experience and asked the Lord to come into my heart. I was excited and experienced a heart change instantaneously. I didn't just feel it, I knew it in my soul.

4) Sensing God's Voice

I have had various occasions where I experienced sensing God speak in my spirit. In the mid '70s I knew in my spirit an acronym for the word faith-Father All's In Thy Hand. I have shared that phrase with others in many ways—on note cards, on bags, on shirts and hats. In 2011, while on my knees quiet before the Lord I sensed one word beating loudly in my heart—the word Covenant. I believe God has sent me on a covenant journey and this writing *The New Heart Matters: A Covenant Journey* is the outcome.

5) My Hope

My hope is to encourage readers to embrace God's power and fellowship found in His covenant of eternal love.

AS A WIDOW

1) "A Thread of Love"

This piece describes how God led Lee and me to live victoriously in our marriage of 50 years, even though there were difficult times and wonderful experiences as well. We learned to walk in unity. We would tell our family and friends that we were one - if Leon did the cooking, then I could be considered cooking too. Our marriage was not always one of peace and harmony. It was the Hand of the Lord (See Isaiah 41:19, 20) that molded and shaped our marriage and made it whole. During the Spring of 2016 my husband died unexpectedly.

God through His Spirit led me to Proverbs 19:21 – "Many are the plans in a man's heart, but God's purpose will prevail." God's peace held me close to His heart. His Presence sustained me. His love was my daily comforter. God's promise was fulfilled for He promised to never leave nor to forsake His children. What love!

A Thread of Love

Leon, my husband, would ask others, "Have I told you our love story and what happened on our first date?" If given a listening ear he would begin, "It was a starry night of bliss and it all started with a kiss!" Three years later we married.

That was 52 years ago. Leon and I became devoted Christians, were faithful and diligent in the work world, raised five children, welcomed 16 grand and great grandchildren as our heritage and experienced both wonderful and difficult times during our marriage. We learned to walk in unity. We would tell our family and friends that we were one - if Leon did the cooking then I could be considered cooking, too. If I made groceries then one could consider Leon as having made the groceries as well. We would say, "We are one"!

Our marriage was not always one of peace and harmony. It was not always peaceful. It was "the Hand of the Lord" (See Isaiah 41:19, 20) that molded and shaped our marriage and made it whole. He brought it out of the "slimy pit, out of the mud and mire and set" it on the Rock (Psalm 40:2 NIV). "Many, Lord my God, are the wonders you have done, the things you planned for us. None can compare with you, were I to speak and tell of your deeds, they would be too many to declare" (Psalm 40:5 NIV).

As I reflect on a day that I was leaving the hospital room where my husband was assigned, after having back surgery late March 2016, I am reminded of several defining experiences. One found Leon and me spreading a love message. It started with me posting a card on the cork board that was on the wall in his room. The card read, "Have I told you I love you today?" This is a question that Leon would ask me at the start of the day. We would try to catch the other by asking the question first. When various staff members would come in his room, Leon would greet them with the love message and they would look surprise and laugh or smile.

The second experience describes what happened as Leon's hospital stay was extended. Now by the fifth day of his hospital stay complications began to set in - pneumonia, a low blood count and the need for a blood transfusion. He was placed in the Intensive Care Unit for a day and was reassigned to another room the following day. A few days later as I was about to leave his room to go home, Leon said, "I sure wish I could wrap you in my arms." I said, "How you are you going to do that?" Then he said, "Can you get up on the bed with me?" I replied, "Can you move over?" Then Lee said, "Can you come tomorrow at 6:00 a.m.?" I said, "How about 9 a.m.?" I kissed him and said, "Love you!"

The next morning my phone rang about 6:30 a.m. It was someone from the hospital who told me that my husband had gone into cardiac arrest. When I arrived at the hospital and walked into Leon's room the doctor was still pumping his chest but it was too late. That was April 5, 2016.

His death was unexpected. He had been admitted to the hospital on Easter Monday, March 28 and had back surgery that morning at 11:00 a.m. The surgery was successful and we were quite hopeful for a smooth recovery. We had made plans for my husband to transition to a local rehabilitation hospital and even knew that room 30 had been reserved for him.

By 11:00 a.m., on the morning of the 5th, most of our children and grandchildren, other relatives and friends had gathered in his room and some at his bedside. A chaplain was there to minister to the family. She and I talked and I shared with her how during the week I had discovered a book, The Power of Prayer by Myles Munroe, on Leon's night stand at home. I had come across a verse that resonated in my spirit which I continued to think about throughout the time Lee was in the hospital. I had failed to remember the reference but had committed the verse to memory.

I quoted the verse and she googled it and found Proverbs 19:21 "Many are the plans in a person's heart, but it is the Lord's purpose that prevails (NIV)." As mentioned before, we had plans for Leon to be admitted to the rehabilitation center but God called him home.

The final defining experience that I want you to share is how God's peace kept me during such an unexpected time of loss. I believe God's Word, "You, Lord give true peace to those who depend on you, because they trust you" (Isaiah 26:3, NCV) and I put my trust in You, God. God promises to grant sleep to those He loves (Psalm 127:2).

It has been a little over a year ago since my husband passed and God has granted me sleep continuously. All things are possible to those who believe and so I believe that God made it possible for me to experience His peace that is above all that one can comprehend.

I continue to dwell in Jesus, for in him I live and move and have my being (Acts 17:28). It's the power of his life in us that releases peace, love, joy and all we need to live victoriously.

God allowed Lee and me to live victoriously in our marriage unity and He sprinkled it with threads of love. Leon captured a great truth based on God saying He loves us (Jeremiah 31:3) and now our family, friends and others have embraced his message, "HAVE I TOLD U I LOVE YOU TODAY?" Pass it on!

—Lorraine Kelley Flood

May 12, 2017

2) 37th Anniversary Thought

This 37th anniversary writing tells how Lee and I worked together to the very end of thirty seven years and were blessed in various ways. These blessings included having a lovely family; learning not to be selfish but to seek the good of others; blessed with a home not just a house and the focus on the idea of living together in oneness.

God Has Made Us One

July 7,2000

Lee,

The best thing that you can give me today is 37 years. Do you know how wonderful this is? It is something that we should be very proud of—working together to the very end of thirty-six years.

Now, let's consider what we have been blessed with for 37 years.

God has blessed us with each other and from this Holy union we have a lovely family—actually, a nation. This was always His plan. We declare that we are His children. He has given us His Holy Spirit. The Holy Spirit leads us and guides us all the days of our lives and through eternity. We should never fear for "love" casts out all fear. God has shown us how to love each other—for He is love.

He has shown us "not to seek our own good, but the good of others." To show others that we love them is much harder than telling them. So God knew to bless us with children to love—five beautiful gifts—godly offspring. He has given them His Spirit. He promised that He would put His word in the mouths of our children and our children's children. How blessed we are to be able to tell others that God has saved our children. They all will be—God promised! What an awesome God! What a great reason to celebrate our 37 years.

Look how God has blessed us with a "home" not just a house. The word declares "except God builds the home, we labor in vain." One great thing about this home is that we welcome others as a sign of our hospitality. This is for God's glory!

Another gift that comes along with our thirty-seven years is the very "stuff" that holds us together—oneness. We are one & we know it. This, to me, is the secret to a successful marriage—unity. Malachi 2 describes the purpose of marriage—"Has not the Lord made them one? In flesh and Spirit they are His—because He was seeking godly offspring." God made this marriage. What an awesome God we serve.

Dear Heart, Lee, make no mistake about these 37 years– b and the many more to come, they belong to God. He has made us one for His glory!

3) "Have I Told U I Love You Today?" Poem

Words to encourage others to embrace the saying Leon would say, "Have I Told u I Love You Today?"

To family and friends, Remember this day,

It has embers of flames, To light what you say.
You know the question, Leon would share,

I've passed it to you, Now show that you care.

Say it to family, Say it to friends, Say it
to others, Love always wins!

Rekindled friendship, From years gone past.
Has embers of light, Upon love has been cast.
You know the question, Leon would share,

I passed it to you, Now show that you care.

Say it to family, Say it to friends, Say it
to others, Love always wins!

4) Lee's Legacy Day Poem

This poem tells how "Lee's Legacy Day" was born.

LEE'S LEGACY DAY

One year ago today, Lee's legacy was born. For
it's the day Our God called him home.

April the 5th - Lee's Legacy Day.

We named it that very way.

Because he would say "Have I told you, I love you, today?"

Such a warm and endearing memory,

Yes, that was Lee's way.

He left us with this legacy gift To pass along life's way,

For this he would ask at home and many places,
Oh, the smiles that appeared up on their faces!

It's full of life and fun to tell,

Let's help to make the whole world well!

So on today, we rejoice In many and various ways,

We join with family and friends, As we celebrate

LEE'S LEGACY DAY!

April 5, 2017

AS A MOTHER

"THE GIFT OF LOVE: BUNDLED TOGETHER IN FAMILY"

1) God's Gift to Us: The Family

This poem is based on Genesis 2:24 which points out the coming together of the man and woman in oneness and out of this oneness godly offspring can be raised. For us this gift is the Flood family. This is the gift God gave to us our family. In this poem I lay out the characteristic of each family member beginning with Lee Sr. symbolizing love and each child representing the fruit of our marital love.

The Flood Family Legacy

I will pour out my Spirit on your offspring and my blessings on your descendants. Isaiah 44:3

God's Gift to Us: The Family

And this is the gift God gave to us

The Flood Family

Lee, my husband, symbolizes LOVE,

And this is the fruit of OUR LOVE:

The first born, Andrea, is STRENGTH

The second child, Lee Jr., is TRUTH

The third child, LaVaughan, is FAITH

The fourth child, Adrienne, is CARE

The fifth child, Allison, is COMMITMENT

MotherDear is PATIENCE.

Aleyshia, the first born grandchild, is CONFIDENCE.

And the other seeds contain, EVERLASTING LIFE:

James III, Jerrell, Terrell, Andre, Jordan, Robyn,

Alvin III, Daniel, Jayda, Aaron, and April.

God gave us the gift of LOVE. All bundled
together in FAMILY.

As inspired by Lorraine, The Wife,

The Mother, The Grandmother, and The Daughter!

(1998)

The family crest was designed in 2009 by Allison. This coat of arms represents the importance we place on a Christian home where peace reigns. The color green represents Eternal Life and the blue color represents the Water of Life-Christ Jesus. The fleur-de-lis, the design (at the top of the shield) in the form of three tapering petals tied by a surrounding band, usually represents Christianity. This shield represents our Christian family.

2) A Thank You Note from Mother

This letter addressed to my five children expresses my appreciation to them for my 75th surprise birthday celebration. They planned it all and executed it well.

Ann, Lee Jr., LaVaughan, A, and Alli,

As I reflect on my 75th surprised birthday celebration that you planned and executed so beautifully, I think – "Though the celebration is over, the joy of it continues on forever". So you have given me an everlasting experience that could only have been birth out of the depths of your love for me.

Now speaking of love, that's what was spread to all who came to this awesome affair. In order to spread this love it has to be in you and we all know that it is so. Your love allowed you to work together as family and others could sense it. That's powerful!

Joy and happiness permeated the atmosphere. There was movement and laughter; dancing and Andrea singing; talking and eating. The guests gave gifts and you served food and it was delicious. The decorations gave the place an ambience of elegance. Then there was cake – "icinged" with green symbolizing life (You know me!) The photographer took pictures, a thousand, I believe, worth "many" a word - pictures of me and you, the FIVE; me and my siblings and their spouses; me and both generation of grands; me and other kin folk; me and my friends; me, Joyce and Costella; me and Lionel.

We danced - me with each of you and me and my dance partner, Joe and each of you read a portion of the song, "Sweet Lorraine" - typed in a flower garden and framed in gold. This choice was quite significant because this was the song that inspired Mother Dear to name me 75 years ago.

You all appeared happy - my impressively beautiful daughters and my sons confident, stylish and just plain handsome. Smart at that, as well, and best of all, you know how to make things happen and you did!

What a magnificent celebration that ended with long stem glasses filled with sparkling champagne - the grand toast lead by the firstborn son - then a series of light ringing sounds!

To you all, I AM GRATEFUL! Love you forever,
Your Mother

A Gratitude of Thanks for MotherDear

O Lord, with a heart of gratitude,
We are thankful for our MotherDear,
For the love that she surely shared,
During the time that she had here.

I asked her, one special day,
Of the words that she would leave,
I'm thankful for her answer.
Now, that same we can achieve.

The same level of her long-lived life,
Long-lasting and free,
This family, we can do this,
Be loving – Be free.

So, now with this freedom,
That Fannie did instill,
Let me tell you what she told me,
Let me tell, what she revealed.

She said, tell my children,
That they were truly loved,
Tell them somebody really loved them
From me and God above.

Tell them, tell the children,
Pass it all along,
Tell the next generation,
That love to them belong.

Now you embrace this treasure,
You embrace this pearl,
It's simply this and nothing else.
Love should rule our world.

MotherDear did embody this,
Through her many-many days,
If and when you met her,
You would remember her loving ways.

This Fannie is free-spirited.
This Fannie, sometimes a mess.
This Fannie, we all love her,
MotherDear, The Best!

AS A MEMA (GRANDMOTHER)

1) Marriage I, II, III

In a personal note, before my granddaughter, Aleyshia, got married, she asked me a question regarding being married. I told her that I believe at the core of marriage is "forgiveness". (See my thoughts about marriage in three parts.)

Marriage Part I: Marriage and My Upbringing

Aleyshia, if you know me, then you must know that I view marriage from a Christian perspective. There are three factors that have shaped my beliefs regarding marriage -my upbringing, personal experiences and the Word.

First, let me tell you about growing up during the 1940s and the 1950s. We had a tight-knit family and lived in a tight-knit community. The majority of our adult family members were married. The majority of the households in our neighborhood included married couples with children. I grew up going to church. All around me at church were families that included moms and dads that were married. The culture that I grew up in was made up of families which included married couples with children. I was shaped by my environment-people, place and things. When I was finishing 12th grade, one of my friends interviewed me and asked me what was I looking forward to in the future. I responded, "I want a family and I want to make my husband happy." I was 17 at that time and had that vision. Last year your granddaddy and I celebrated our 50 years of marriage. I will point you to a letter that I wrote to the editor of The Virginian-Pilot in 2007 entitled "7-7-7-7-7-7-7". It points to how we were able to overcome the "devil" of miscommunication by following the advice found in Matthew 18:22. I believe what you find there is the key to relationships. "Forgiveness."

Marriage Part II: Marriage and My Experiences

Now forgiveness is at the heart of Christianity. You know that we come into the saving grace of Jesus-through forgiveness.

When things are reconciled-we can then fellowship with the Father.

Well it works the same way in marriage. When the couple experiences challenges, hurts, arguments and on and on and on . . . one forgives the other, the forgiveness is received and then they make up. Things are reconciled and you move on.

I believe that forgiveness is a spiritual action and characteristic right from the heart of the Father and we can know it only through Jesus. The reason I say it's only from Jesus is because as Christians we die to ourselves that Jesus might live his life in and through us. Otherwise we live our own selfish lives. Forgiveness is hardly in our thoughts and therefore, we hardly forgive and truly make up.

Long-lasting marriages are built on the premise of "forgiveness & making-up." Making-up is hard to do without its partner forgiveness- which is Jesus. Jesus is forgiveness and He, Forgiveness, lives in us. With that said, we can forgive any and every thing that's done against us. I believe this. I know this.

Marriage Part III: Marriage and the Word

There are familiar verses in the Bible (the Word) that most people know and often use when referring to family-matters

"Train up a child in the way he should go …"; "Husbands love your wives as Christ loves the church."; and "Children obey your parents. . . ." But the Word that has greatly influenced me most regarding the family-matter of marriage is found in Malachi 2:15 that points to the purpose of marriage.

From the Message version – "God, not you, made marriage. His Spirit inhabits even the smallest details of marriage. And what does He want from marriage?"

From the New International Version - (I like this version) "Has not the Lord made them one? In flesh and spirit they are

His. And why one? Because He was seeking godly offspring. So guard yourself in your spirit."

Aleyshia I believe that marriage is a spiritual partnership. When there is intimacy -oneness- so much is poured into each other.

There is giving and receiving; there is peace and joy; there is celebration and jubilation; there are soft voices and sensual moans; and it's godly fruit-godly offspring.

The Word declares that marriage is a mystery. Only God can reveal the truth of that mystery.

To the Praise of His Glory!

lkflood

April 15,2014

2) Dear Grandchildren

This letter was written to my grandchildren in November 2008 on this historic day when Barack Obama became the first African American President of the United States of America.

November 4, 2008

Dear Grandchildren,

Today, I am writing to you as an eyewitness to the election of Barack Obama, the first African-American to be elected president in its 232-year history. While it was such a magnificent event, its significance is of greater thought. Let me tell you why. Do you remember that Dr. Martin Luther King, Jr. spoke about the dream of his children not being judged by the color of their skin but rather by the content of their character? Well, he wanted his children to have an equal opportunity in America as was promised in the Constitution. He died hoping that one day America would change and today America changed. I witnessed it!

Today, I saw hope come alive when Obama was elected president of the United States of America. When hope showed up, I saw crowds and crowds of people with their hands lifted in celebration. I saw tears flowing down many faces - Jesse and Oprah's - just to name a few. I saw the young, the old, and the bright-and-bushy tail! I saw a myriad of people of varying hues. I heard the noises of jubilation of those gathered as one at Grant Park. This was a sea of hope, with righteousness at its back.

I felt the Spirit of Life—Life that brought action—Life that brought change to America. This is the America where the idea of "limitless possibility" came true, at least for today. On this day, "Yes We Can" came alive for all. The story of America came through Obama's election. America's story of "opportunity, possibility and miracles" returned to our Nation where "God shed his Grace on thee".

So children, get on board and follow the yellow-brick-road of hope and opportunity. Awake from the Dream, for it's a new day in our land. Hope has transformed America because of an Obama victory. Change has come and the whole world saw its entrance. I want you to know that that's significant!

Love, Grandma

P. S. Turn off that TV and get your homework done and don't forget to read everyday. Most of all, love others!

"109 YEARS"

1) The "Ruth and Boaz" Experience: Where Love Abides

A Ruth and Boaz experience is a narrative of my husband, Lionel, and my relational story leading to our marriage after our spouses died in the same month of 2016. We talked, we dated, we married.

"A RUTH AND BOAZ EXPERIENCE"

Lionel, my husband of four years said to me recently, "I'm going to take you someplace you've never been before." He then took my hand and led me to the kitchen. So funny! My goodness, did we laugh! That humor is hidden within Lionel.

That was his way of telling me that I needed more experience cooking. It may have been the truth but he used "a little bit of honey to make the medicine go down."

Sometimes the unexpected ushers in a new experience. Think about how Ruth was led by Naomi to an unexpected new love with Boaz, Naomi's cousin. Ruth was a Moabite woman who had been married to Naomi's son, Mahlon. He died unexpectedly leaving Ruth a widow. She left her homeland with her mother-in-law, Naomi who was also a widow. Ruth told Naomi in these well-known words, "wherever you go I will go; your God will be my God". What loyalty Ruth demonstrated to Naomi. What great character Ruth displayed day in and day out. Boaz recognized Ruth's traits and fell in love with her "because of her character and her heart".

Cora, my friend, was my Naomi. Let me share my story. I became a widow in early April 2016. I had been married for 52 years. Lionel's wife passed away at the end of April 2016. He had been married for 57 years. Cora, Lionel and I had known each other for well over 50 years. He delivered mail at the school where Cora and I shared a classroom together. Lionel's son was in the class where I was assigned to as a student teacher. Lionel was quite sociable and well-liked by the staff. He was also the president of the Parent Teacher Association (PTA) at the school.

In early May 2016 I received a call from Cora sharing with me that Bullock's (as we called him) wife had passed. I read the obituary in the newspaper. Months later I received a call from Lionel offering condolences regarding the passing of my husband. By the Fall of the year, we began to develop a relationship. We began to go to church together; out to lunch and sometimes to dinner. Then we would find time to go to the beach and stroll down the boardwalk and visit friends.

Two years later, we married. Lionel was 83 years old and I was 76. Lionel would share with others that we had a total of 109 years of marriage between us. We found out that we were the oldest couple to be married at my church and vows conducted by Bishop Courtney McBath.

2) Did You Think You Would Ever Love Again?

This birthday message opens with a powerful question that Lionel asked me, "Did you ever think you would love again?" The message includes my response.

May 23, 2018

Happy Birthday!

(3 months before we married)

Lionel, you asked,

"Did you ever think you would love again?"

How lovingly curious you are.

How excitingly are your thoughts - You love quite caring,

Your touch so gentle.

A twinkle in your eyes And such a pleasant smile.

Well liked. Engaging!

You asked, "Would I love again?"

Yes!

YOU!

HAPPY BIRTHDAY!

"This is my covenant with them," says the Lord. "My Spirit will not leave them, and neither will these words I have given you. They will be on your lips and on the lips of your children and your children's children forever. I, the Lord, have spoken."
—ISAIAH 59:21 (NLT)

THE NEW HEART MATTERS!
~IT'S WHERE THE SPIRIT REIGNS!~

www.ingramcontent.com/pod-product-compliance
Lightning Source LLC
Chambersburg PA
CBHW062112080426
42734CB00012B/2832